THE KONKANI PROVERBS

THE KONKANI PROVERBS

V. P. CHAVAN

GYAN

Published by

Gyan Publishing House
5, Ansari Road
Daryaganj, New Delhi-110002
Phone: 011-47034999, 9811692060
E-mail: books@gyanbooks.com

Distribution Network
gyanbooks.com
India, USA, Canada, UK, Australia, France

ISBN : 978-81-212-3671-3 (PB)
First Published, Bombay, 1923

2nd Impression 2020

Printed at: Gyan Press, Delhi.

The book at your disposal is the edition of an old book originally published long back. The Text quality of this book may not be at par as compared to our other books but many readers approached us to reprint this important book so that it could satiate their hunger. We request all the readers of this book to help us to improve its quality by providing the necessary text of those pages which are not properly visible. Your valuable support in this case will be highly appreciated and acknowledged and our future readers will be benefitted immensely.

Respectfully Dedicated

(by permission)

TO

HIS HIGHNESS

SIR SHREE RAJARAM CHHATRAPATI MAHARAJ, G.C.I.E., ETC., ETC.;

THE MAHARAJAH OF KOLHAPORE,

THE NOBLE DESCENDANT

OF THE

GREAT SHRI SHIWAJI MAHARAJ.

यःप्राप्तकालं किल सावधानः ।
करोति कार्यं विषमस्थितोऽपि ।
सिद्धिर्ध्रुवा सत्त्ववतश्च यस्य ।
तमेव सन्तो ब्रुवते महान्तम् ॥

(That man alone is great who rises to the emergencies of the occasion and becomes master of the situation.)

V. P. CHAVAN.

FOREWORD.

By The Rev. JOHN McKENZIE, M.A.,

Principal, Wilson College, Bombay.

President, Anthropological Society of Bombay.

Dr. Chavan is already well-known for his work on the Konkani language, and a large circle of readers will welcome this work on Konkani Proverbs. The proverbs of any people are of enormous value as an aid to the understanding of the people's mind. The Scholar who merely collects them, performs a service of a very high order, but he who not only collects them but explains and illumines them, as Dr. Chavan has done, is deserving of the gratitude of all who are led either by scientific interest or by ordinary human interest to study the ways in which the minds of peoples different from themselves express themselves.

The Proverb is one of the most interesting forms in which the wisdom of peoples has been embodied. It is one of the oldest. Indeed, I believe it and the fable are the oldest forms in which wisdom has been fixed and preserved, so that it has become not merely the passing thought of this or that individual at a given moment but the abiding possession of a whole people for many generations. Proverbs have not depended on the art of writing, still less on that of printing, for their preservation. They have been graven on the minds of men and women. And this has been possible because of three qualities which long ago were pointed out as characteristic of them—shortness, sense, and salt. Dr. Chavan has recognised these qualities as characteristic of all proverbs, as well as a fourth quality, popularity, and he has found them to be characteristic of the proverbs of the Konkan.

I do not think one goes to the proverb if one wishes to find the highest ethical and spiritual thought of a people. One finds in the proverb as in the fable rather principles of worldly prudence than high ethical teaching. As a distinguished living psychologist (Shand, *The Foundations of Character*, p. 78) has said regarding proverbs, " They are matters of advice, of warning, of exhortation, of reproof, of consolation ; but seldom enunciate laws of character." There are many in most languages which belong to even a lower order; many in which the spirit is that of a half-humorous cynicism. The proverb then becomes a whip to scourge folly or vice—and folly more often than vice. The present collection provides abundant illustration of this.

Further, we hardly look in the proverb for scientific precision of statement. We have all from time to time heard a proverb quoted very effectively to clinch a thoroughly unsound argument. It may have been that the proverb expressed a partially true generalisation or it may have been that it contained a statement which was literally true, but which was not really applicable to the situation to which it was secondarily and figuratively applied. One of the most interesting of the series of papers in the *Essays of Elia* is that on Popular Fallacies, in which Lamb takes up a number of popular sayings, most of them proverbs and shows the grave imperfections of the wisdom which they contain. The proverb contains a wisdom which has not reached the rank of philosophy, and we have completely misunderstood its character if we look in it for more than the homely wisdom of the common people. Nevertheless, if we take it for what it is, we shall find in it a wisdom which is worthy of our respect.

I do not propose to discuss the peculiar characteristics of the proverbial sayings which Dr. Chavan has here gathered together. We find in them, the characteristics that mark the proverb everywhere and at all times, and we find light in them to guide us in the understanding of many of the characteristics of Konkani thought and life. He has presented them so that those of us who know no Konkani may read them and understand them for ourselves, and I shall only say again that he is deserving of our gratitude for his valuable work.

PROVERBS IN KONKANI LANGUAGE.

By Rao Saheb Dr. V. P. Chavan, L.M. & S.

Proverbs and their place in Anthropology.

Proverbs are considered to be a form of Folk-literature or its later imitators, expressing in the form of a simple, homely sentence, a pungent criticism of life. Proverbs are sometimes, valuable, ethical precepts which have kept high ideals before the masses. On the other hand, there are proverbial sayings, accepted by the masses, which are very pernicious in their influence. For instance, "Every man has his price" &c. Among Orientals, proverbs form the foundations of moral and political philosophy. They have a special influence in impressing upon the minds of the masses fundamental principles of morality and noble living.

Proverbs are as old as the world. From the Vedas down to the holy Books of the Christians and the Mohamedans, the proverbs have been exercising a peculiar sway over mankind professing different religions and persuasions. These proverbs, in fact, go back to the infancy of the races and civilizations. They are to be found in the literary remains of Babylonia and Egypt. Even the savages of primitive times, have had their proverbs. In fact, it would not be wrong to assume that the proverbs themselves have succeeded in moulding the varying characters of different nations. In Sanskrit, we have got a book called the Sarangadhar Paddhati of the 14th century containing 6,000 verses culled from 264 different authors.

Proverbs—how formed.

Proverbs are shaped by spontaneous utterances inspired by some incident or happenings that stirred the imagination. The following which I have culled from a well-known source, will illustrate, in a forcible manner, how a trivial incident resulted into a pithy saying that has succeeded in exerting a potent influence over a great mass of people.

> "The popular proverb "When you go to Rome, do as "Rome does," is an interesting instance of how an "aphorism may grow out of an incident which was "subsequently forgotten. Few, who use it, know "that it had its origin in connection with Monica, the "mother of Saint Augustine. As the Sabbath was a "feast day in Milan according to prevailing Roman "usage but a fast at her native place of Tagaste, Monica "was perplexed as to her course, and her conscience "troubled her. Saint Ambrose, however, settled the "case of Conscience by uttering the oft-quoted adage."
>
> गांवा सारको भेस गुरू सारको उपदेस.

Mixed with sense and some teaching, the proverb spreads with authority and forces its acceptance by its very truth. They also grow up from riddles or may be summed up as a quintessence of a well-known fable. It will be interesting to note that rough-hewn proverbs go an adding additional lustre and polish as they travel from one language to another and then to the third and so on.

Four Qualities necessary.

They say four qualities are necessary to constitute a proverb. (1) Brevity or conciseness; (2) Sense; (3) Piquancy and (4) Popularity. All these four are to be found in the Konkani proverbs. Although piquancy is its chief characteristic, these short pithy sayings in Konkani dialect do manage to convey serious thoughts. They show the peculiar characteristics of the people, whose mother-tongue it has been, presenting their ideals of Life and conduct. They are, also, full of pungent criticisms on our daily life, with an eye to teach us the best way with which to fight the worries of our mundane existence. They do this by fixing our attention on their amusing wit. Without popularity these sayings would die a natural death. In short, a proverb must be a house-hold word, a sort of "spontaneous growth out of the soil of national character."

Trustworthy witnesses.

The Konkani proverbs not only abound in certain figures of speech but they are impressive as well. The hyper-bole and the paradox are to be found in them, like the English proverb "No answer is also an answer". Our Konkani proverbs have got a local form and colour, which add to their popularity and potent influence. This very influence on the general mass of people turns them—the proverbs into trustworthy witnesses of the religious, social, nay, even the political ideals of the peoples who use them.

Among the many who have helped me, it will be invidious to select a few but all the same I cannot but express my thanks to my friend Shanai Wamanbâb Varde Valavalikar, a well-known scholar of Konkani, who has helped me not only by contributing a good many proverbs but has also taken a good deal of trouble in going with me over the proverbs especially those sent over by my young and energetic friend Mr. S. G. Naik of Travancore.

Many of the Gowd Saraswat families went over to Travancore side and settled there, some five or six hundred years ago. Circumstances forced them, not only to adopt the local language —Malayalam—but the local manners, customs and the local religion—Vaishnavism as well. In spite of adverse and often critical conditions, these Brahmins have succeeded in maintaining themselves as a separate entity. They are in a flourishing condition and have kept up their connection with their old tutelary Gods in Goa. It is a matter of admiration also, that they have continued the use of their mother tongue, the old, old dialect of Konkani, all these hundreds of years. The proverbs in use, there, show however, a good many peculiarities, often un-intelligible to people on this side. One does not know whether these proverbs reveal the original form of Konkani or they have been modified more or less by long their contact with Malayalam. I have put down these proverbs with an equivalent in parenthesis.

The difficulties.

The difficulties of collecting the sayings and proverbs of a language which is merely a spoken one, are immense. The economic factor, besides, is producing the greatest rot in the life-history of the language. It is used in Bombay, no doubt, but you have to search far, for the families who use it in their circles to convey or express their thoughts among themselves But the difficulties do not end here. For even those who use it are not in a position to decide with authority the particular shade of the meaning attached to a proverb, in the absence of standard books and writers, which alone are the final authorities to accord a definite place to a definite saying. But it is the ladies, strong in their conservatism, that have come to my help and have decided the meaning of some of these proverbs with a decision, often lacking in their husbands. With all that, there are some proverbs which have to be left to their own fate without any explanation.

Help from the ladies.

I am not exaggerating as regards the help I got from these ladies. There is one proverb जोर रडा खैं पेजेक. *The fever cries for conjee* is the literal translation. But none of my friends could make out what particular sense it conveyed. Different people put on different construction and that is why the proverb was submitted to a lady. She laughed. " Oh ! Ye ! Simpletons", said she ! " It is no wonder that you could not understand the saying simply because you have caught hold of the wrong half of it." It is जोर रडा खैं पेजेक घैरत्र रडा खैं जागेक. " *The fever cries for not getting the conjee and the cob-web cries for not getting any room to spread itself.*"

" Once it so happened," continued the lady, " that there was a battle royal as to their respective superiority between the fever and the cob-web. The fever insisted that he was the superior person and the cob-web must bow to him. Even the mighty kings fall down prostrate when the fever visits them. No, you are wrong, replied the cob-web. I am the all pervading one. I am to be found not only in the palaces of the Kings but in big forests as well. No place in the wide, wide world is free from my presence. How to decide the superiority was the question. And they were obliged to settle it by their own efforts. The cob-web went to the King's palace and spread himself there but the servants were too wide awake to allow him to remain there. He was brushed off. In the meanwhile the fever visited a poor man. The man being very poor, there was not even the conjee to quench the thirst produced by the fever and so the fever was starved out. Both the cob-web and the fever were in a similar predicament. Practically it was a question of the kettle calling the tea-pot black!"

Rude and unpolished but pithy and terse.

A close study of the Konkani proverbs, reveals the traits that are peculiar to us all Indians, no doubt. These proverbs, however, show that they were in existence at a time when the country was not high up in civilized manners and polite speech. Konkani proverbs make use of all parts of the human body to drive the sense home. The idea underlying the proverb "रेड्या गांडी कडेन किनरी" which means playing the flute near the buttocks of the buffalo, is expressed in a more polite way in a Marathi proverb "गाढवा पुढें वाचली गीता" the Holy Gita was read before a donkey. Both express the utter helplessness of either the buffalo or the donkey deriving any benefit, religious or mental from the performance. But one is clothed in Nature's garment and the other is dressed in an up-to-date attire. Another proverb पॉंविळ्यांत मुतूंक बरें means a leak in the roof of the house, allowing the rain water to come in. If a man makes water in that puddle, nobody is the wiser and it is convenient also. But there is a deeper significance attached to this proverb. If there be any scandal in the house, one should not add to it by his own action. What it really means is that one should not urinate in the house, even if there be a puddle there. पादाक नांव परमेश्वर is another rude but pithy proverb, meaning that when a rich man does anything nasty, he is praised instead of being taken to task. दुबळ्याक × × भोंव and देवाची गेली घांट जाल्यार पुजाऱ्याचें गेलें × × are other examples of the same type.

These and many other proverbs similarly worded show that when proverbs of such rude and unpolished type were in vogue, the state of the society was not high up in the scale of polished manners. Besides, when a language gets elevated to the written characters it manages to absorb added lustre and polish not only from its prose writers but from its poets as well. The latter bring to it grace and beauty and adorn it with many a jewel born of their genius. The want of literature in the Konkani language due to the then disturbed condition of the society, did not allow the Konkani dialect to get the necessary finishing touches.

The Marathi proverbs, on the other hand, may not be so pithy and touching but they are undoubtedly smooth and polished, shining with a peculiar grace of their own and fit for use in the drawing room.

The terse but uncouth Subhashita.

This shows that the Konkani dialect must have been in existence a good many centuries before the Marathi language came into general use. The Gowd Saraswat Brahmins, whose mother-tongue it has been, are in no way inferior in mental and intelligent culture to the rest of the Brahmins in the whole of India. The community that has produced the Bhandarkars, the Pandits, the Telangs, the Chandavarkars and other mighty giants of intellectual calibre, dare not be considered in any way lower in the then general culture more than a thousand years ago. The uncouthness of the proverbs must be, therefore attributed to the then state of the society. The Sanskrit poets, not excluding the towering Kalidas, are full of direct allusions to the different anatomical parts of the body. I remember very well a verse from the Subhashita:—

" May you have the joy and pleasure, Oh! Mighty King! said the Brahmin which we derive after thoroughly scratching the ringworm affecting the thighs and especially the adjacent parts and may your enemies have that sort of insufferable agony, which one experiences when one is unable to scratch the part when the itch is on!

Note also another blessing राजन् तव यशो भाति वृद्ध ब्राम्हण शष्पवत्.

This sort of blessing is very pithy and to the point. In the stress of life and worries of our existence, we do manage to forget many a sweet and fragrant blossom out of the Sanskrit literature. But these rude and unpolished but true-to-the-life proverbs or Subhashits have their permanent effect on our train of thought. That is why they succeed better in moulding our character and find a permanent place in our mental make-up.

I would like to draw particular attention to some of the proverbs, just to show what a charming and interesting subject it is, which gives us an insight into the various factors that have made us what we are.

Ages of a man.

Let us take the different ages of man, each of which has got its appropriate proverbs. पांच नागडो नाच. We allow our children to run practically naked, till they are five. This proverb sets a seal on that custom.

धा जायतें खा. It is no use preventing a child from enjoying the sort of food and sweets, it goes in for. This proverb allows full liberty in eating to the children upto the age of 10.

वीस करता खिसमीस. Well, a young virile man of 20 goes in for love songs. It is the premonitory fluttering when the heart seems to thrill within you, like some baby bird singing its first song.

साट बुद्ध नाट. Indians grow old very soon. And a man aged sixty is expected to be imbecile.

णोव आंडाक चोय. When a man attains the age of 90, he is so much bowed down that his eyes approach the thighs.

The mild Hindu.

The mild Hindu takes an exaggerated view of the preservation of Life and tries to turn himself into a soft putty like mass. उबो आस मेरेन लाखाचो, मरून कुच फुकाचो. As long as the man is alive, he is worth a lakh of rupees. No sooner he dies, he is worth nothing. Further manual work is considered low. दाय आसताना हात लासचो न्हव. Why work when you have servants. The result being चोराच्या भयान धेतलॅं रान, थैं मेळ्ळो मुसलमान, ताणें कापले नाख कान. A man ran to the Jungles, being afraid of the thief. There he came across a Mahomedan who cut off his nose and ears. Then we philosophize. एक दिस मांयलो, एक दिस सुनेलो. Ah! Our day will also come. This puts some courage in us and make us think आपले सांवळ्येक आपुण भियेता why should we be afraid of our own shadows? But we conveniently forget आपली सांवळी आपल्या पांयां मुळा that we create our own shadows. Goodness gracious! The last proverb केल्लीं कर्मां ह्याच जल्मा shows that we have to suffer and reap the fruits of our actions in this very life. All these proverbs sum up the Hindu as he is to-day.

One thing more. When this book was ready for the press, I heard for the first time that the late Rev. Dr. Dalgado had published, a good many Konkani proverbs in Portuguese in the city of Lisbon some 25 years ago. It may be so. None of us—and my friends have tried hard all these three years,—has ever come across any book relating to these proverbs. This will be seen from my lame efforts in elucidating the inner meaning of many of those proverbs given here.

With these few general remarks I turn to the subject proper. But before I do so, I cannot but place one thing before you and that is my inability to do full justice to the subject for lack of literary materials. I cannot but re-echo the Sanskrit poet who said "यन्मो ज्ञातम् तदपि अल्पम् अज्ञातं बहुलं भुवि." (What we know is very little but what we are ignorant of, is immense.)

THE KONKANI PROVERBS. कोंकणी म्हणण्यों.

1. अडेचो जोगी, कट्ट्यो मुद्रा. One who is a false ascetic will put on cocoanut shell ear-rings *i.e.*, pretenders put on false appearances. Something like गोमुख व्याघ्र सात्विक or बोके संन्यासी.

2. अंथणांतुलो घायु. The ulcer in a private part of the body. Being ashamed, one cannot inform others of one's condition but one cannot also remain quiet as the ulcer is getting foul and offensive. Used when a man is in a difficult position.

3. अर्धा माडार चडून हात सोडचे न्हयत. If you climb up half the cocoanut tree and if you let go your hands, the result will be disastrous. Do not give up heart when you have progressed half the way.

4. अप्पे खंवका की फोंड मेज्जुका ?

(हेलापे खांवक कि फोंड मेजूंक ?)

Do you want to eat the sweet *appe* (a sort of cake) or to count the moulds in the pan in which they are baked?

5. अज्ये तेरावो मोणुयी जालो; घारी खेल्ली मोण्यी जाली.

(आजये-तेरावो म्हणून जालो; घारयो खाल्यो म्हणून जाल्यो)

To get the satisfaction of having performed the 13th day funeral ceremony after the grand-mother's death as well as of having eaten the *gharis*, a sort of sweet dish prepared in connection with the same. Two at one blow or two birds at one shot.

अवळा मंडे विक्किल्ले दुडु खोर्ज्जुंखवना.

(आंवाळे विकून आइल्ले दुडु खोर्जुखायनात)

Money obtained by selling emblic myrabolans does not sting. These myrabolans produce a sort of acrid and disagreeable taste in the mouth; but the money obtained by selling them is of as good a value as ever; similarly any work which provides one with honest remuneration, should not be considered as below one's dignity.

7. अशोंय म्हणचें न्हंय, तशोंय म्हणचें न्हंय; दिवाळेचे दिवे रे पुता.

Neither this is correct nor that is false, like the lamps of Divali. These lights burn for a while and then there is complete darkness. It may be that the paper lamps or Chinese lanterns lighted during the Divali holidays are kept very high. They are of no use to any one. Similar is the case with a man who has no settled opinion.

8. आकैचें काजळ, बाकैचो शेन्दूर. She brought collyrium from the village Akai and red powder from the village of Bakai. This means that she managed to finish her toilet by some means or other. Cf. धर्मावर सोमवार.

9. आंग उदकान नितंळ, मन सतान नितंळ. As the body is purified by water, so is the mind purified by the truth.

10. आंग भिजल्याबगर नुस्तें धरूं नजे. You cannot catch fish unless you enter water. You cannot have pleasures for asking. You have to toil and run risks. Cf. खटपट करी तो पोट भरी. दळील तोच भरील. श्रमाविण फळ नाहीं. नाळाविण कढ नाहीं.

11. आजो गेलो माचो रितो जालो. When the grand-father dies his bedstead is empty. It may mean, nobody to fill up the gap of the old experienced man.

12. आडांग्याचें मडें पादत, धुम्याचें मडें गाजत. People should not do things that are against the usual customs. The Dhume family take their dead to the burning ghat with a good deal of unnecessary noise, whereas the dead body of a stupid man passes wind on its way to the cemetery. आडदांड जातो पादत आणि धुम्या जातो गाजत.

13. आदावाबगर बुडकुलो फोडा ? Nobody cares to spend unless he expects to get some profit.

14. आनाचो भाव दादा. Just as the elder brother is good for nothing, the one elder than him is equally useless. Birds of the same feather. अण्णाचा भाऊ दादा. बडा भाईसे बडा भाई छोटा भाईसे सुभान अल्ला.

15. आपली सांवळी आपल्या पांयांमुळा. One treads one's own shadow. Our actions follow us wherever we may go.

16. आपले सांवळेक आपुण भियेता. To be afraid of one's own shadow. Do not be too nervous. सावळीस भ्याला व भुतास बिलगला. वाजे पाऊल आपुलें, म्हणे मार्गे कोण आलें, रामी रामदास ह्मणे भितो आपणा आपण.

17. आपलो कोयतो हातार बसल्यार नाल्लाक कित्याक गाळी ? When cutting open a cocoanut with a scythe, if the scythe cuts your hand, why abuse the cocoanut ? Blame thyself for thy carelessness. आत्मैव रिपुरात्मनः Cf. नाचतां येईना तर आंगण वांकडें or रांधतां येईना, ओलीं लांकडें.

18. आपलो पांय आपल्या माथ्यार. Keeping one's foot over one's own head, *i.e.*, being ruled over by people who are low and inferior. धन्याचें नांव गण्या, नोकराचें नांव रुद्राजीबुवा.

19. आपली भेस सुण्याक दिवन सुण्याची भेस आपणें घेतल्यार जाता ? If we give over our dress to the dog and put on ourselves the dress of a dog, it would be ridiculous. Nobody should forego his self-respect and identify himself with mean people.

20. आपलो हात जगन्नाथ. Self-help is the best way of leading life in this world. आत्मैव ह्यात्मनो बंधुः Man is the architect of his own fortune. आपला हात आणि जगन्नाथ. But the meaning is quite contradictory in Marathi wherein it means that in case one gets some power, he should utilize it in aggrandizing himself and nobody else.

21. आपल्याल्या पांयांमुळा कुंवाळें कुसलां; दुसऱ्यालीं सांसवां वेंचता. A cucumber lies rotten at one's feet; why should this person pick up a mustard seed at other's feet ? We can see the mole in our brother's eye, but cannot see the beam in our own. आपल्या डोळ्यांतलें मुसळ दिसत नाहीं परंतु दुसऱ्याच्या डोळ्यांतील कुसळ दिसतें. Cf. Prov. No. 550.

22. आपुण आपणाक, देव समस्तांक. Man looks to himself while God looks to all. Everybody for himself while the God is for us all.

23. आपुण मेल्याबगर सर्ग दिसना. We cannot ascend to heaven unless we ourselves die. We cannot have the highest bliss unless we exert ourselves. आपण मेल्यावांचून स्वर्ग दिसत नाहीं.

24. आपुण रांड शिनाळें जाल्यार भावा–बायले पातयेना. When a woman is herself a bad character, she keeps a watch over her brother's wife. Those that are sinful, are watchful about other's sins. Cf. आंधळ्यासी जग सारेंची आंधळें. तुका ह्मणें शुद्ध नाहीं जो आपण, तया त्रिभुवन अवघें खोटें.

25. आंबट खाल्ल्याच्या ताळ्याकडेन जळटा. Same as आंबुस खाल्ल्याळें गळ्यांत कचरता.

26. ओंबुस खाल्ल्यालें गळ्यांत कचरता. If you eat sour things, you will have nausea or feel sourish. Meaning if you have done a wrong, the least reference, even in an indirect way upsets you. आंबट खाल्यावर घशांत खवखवतें. खाई त्याला खवखवे.

27. आंबो पणसांत न्हंय, दुबळो मनशांत न्हंय. The mango cannot be classed among jack fruits, and a poor man cannot be included in the ranks of well-to-do people.

28. आंब्याच्या रुखाक पंगाऱ्याची साल लागता ? The bark of *Pangara* tree cannot be grafted on a mango tree. Another's child cannot be yours, *i.e.*, an adopted child cannot after all have the same affection for its new parents and vice-versa. वडाची साल पिंपळास लागत नाहीं.

29. आमा–लग्नाक मीठ वाळ्ळोलो.

(आवैच्या लग्नाक मीठ वाढिल्लो)

One who has served salt at the wedding dinner of his mother's marriage. This means one who considers himself wiser and more clever than his parents.

30. आमी तुमगेर जेंवक येतात, तुमी आमगेर आंबे धाडात. I will oblige you by coming to dine with you and you may return the obligation by sending me mangoes. This is a typical instance of selfishness. तुमचें तें आमचें व आमचें तें आमच्या बापाचें.

31. आमी तुमी एकां, शितान केलीं लोकां. We are all one but because we cannot provide food for each other, we are separated. Men might join but self-interest drives them apart. यूयं वयं वयं यूयमित्यासीन्मतिरावयोः, किं जातमधुना येन यूयं यूयं वयं वयम् । तुह्मी आह्मी एक कंठाळीला मेख.

32. आयतनांतुलो दिवो.

(आयदनांतलो दिवो)

The light inside a pot. The light of a lamp placed inside a pot will not show light outside the pot .The light can be seen only inside the pot. If a person is very learned and that person does not make use of his learning to teach others, we say that that person is just like a light inside a pot.

33. आयली दिवाळी आनी परबो आकारी. Here is the Divali and let us go on counting other feasts that come in afterwards. This is in reference to a man who wants to enjoy the good things of life all throughout his existence.

34. आयल्यार पावस नाजाल्यार ओत. This shows indifference of the man. Both rain and sun-shine are the same to him. हेंही बरें तेंही बरें.

35. आलेसा, ताण रे बोले, हांव तर भुरगो मुँ गा; आलेसा, जेंवक यो रे, हांव मानाय मुँ गा. Aleixo, pull the oars—and he says, "I am a boy and cannot." Aleixo, come to dine—and he says, "I am a man and can do full justice." Some people would shun duty when it is laborious; yet they would be the first to enjoy the fruit when others toil and procure it. जेवणास आर्धी, निजण्यास मधीं व कामास कधीं मधीं.

36. आंवाळो दिवन कुंवाळो घेवप. To exchange a small emblic myrabolan for a good pumpkin. To get something useful and valuable for an insignificant thing. Cf. Prov. No. 162.

37. आवुस्सुं नात्तिलें चेर्डु पोट्टारें.
(आवै नाथिलें चेडूं पोटारें.)

A motherless child is greedy. It is so simply because it does not know when it will be given another meal.

38. आवैक पळीन धुवेक व्हर, दूद पळोंन म्हशीक व्हर. Look at the mother before you marry the daughter and test the quality and quantity of milk before you go in for a buffalo. Do not go by appearances merely. All is not gold that glitters.

39. आवै जेंवक वाडिना, बापुय भीक मागूंक दिना. The mother does not feed the child and the father does not allow it to beg

One cannot have things both the ways. There must be an allowance on one side at least. आई जेऊं घालीना व बाप भीक मागूं देईना.

40. आवै–बापूय सोडूं येत; पुण शेजारी–सामारी सोडूं येता ? You may perchance desert parents, but not neighbours. You cannot live without the company of good neighbours.

41. आवै मरता धुवे कडेन, धूव मरता गांवच्या मिंडाकडेन. The mother is too loving to her daughter, and the daughter is loving and is attached to her paramour. There is sometimes no return for one's love and attachment. धिक् तांच तंच मदनंच इमांच मांच ।

42. आवै मरूं मावशी उरूं. Let mother die, but let mother's sister live. Rather difficult to explain. It may be that the mother combines love with discipline but the aunt is over-fond. The proverb माय मरो व मावशी जगो also in Marathi shows that if anybody is to die let the mother go. Very filial indeed!

43. आशिळें नाशिळें म्हुने गायरीं, ह्याका खैंचीं सोयरीं-धायरीं ? Whatever I get is not sufficient for my own requirements and how can I think of relatives and friends ? All I get is mine; I do not care for my relations.

44. आळशाक दुणो (दोडो) वात्र, किर्पिणाक दुणो (दोडो) खर्च. The lazy man has to toil double and the miser also has to spend twice as much. Penny-wise and pound-foolish. आळशा दुणें काम लोभ्या दुणा खर्च.

45. आळशाक दुपेट वात्र. The idle man has to do things twice, *i.e.*, the lazy man does things so very carelessly that he has to toil again and again to do his work properly. आळशा दुणें काम.

46. आळशाक भिकणों भाज म्हळीं; तो म्हण्टा, हरवीं खाल्यार चेड बरीं. If you tell a lazy man to bake jack-fruitnuts, he will say,

you can enjoy them better, raw, *i.e.*, the lazy man avoids doing the right sort of things and takes pleasure in doing things in a hap-hazard way.

47. आळशी उठूंक शिवरें शिंकलें. The lazy man gets up to do some work and there is the ill-omen of a noseless man sneezing. Those who do not want to do a thing, want only excuses to run away from the paths of duty. न करत्याचा वार शनिवार.

48. आळशी सांगत तें घाडयाच्या बापायच्यान सांगू नजे. Even the Ghadi's father cannot say what an idle man would say. Lazy people talk big things but do nothing. Ghadi is correctly speaking the exorciser of the devil.

49. इंद्रा मारुथार चंद्राक लागता. The moon gets annoyed if God Indra is beaten. The particular significance of this proverb is difficult to understand. There is hardly any connection even in Mythology between Indra, the God of Gods, and the Moon a third rate deity. Cf. Prov. No. 552.

50. ईन मीन साडेतीन or सवायतीन. All put together only 3½. Very very few. ही = she. मी = I. न means one son and one daughter.

51. उज्जो मळारी आंग लासत्ता वे !

(उजो म्हळ्यार आंग लासता न्हंय !)

Does the mere utterance of the word fire burn ones body ? विस्तव हा शब्द उच्चारिला म्हणून आंग भाजतें काय !

52. उज्याक गेल्यार कैलेक पातयेना. When you go to neighbour's to get some embers for kindling the fire at your own place, the neighbour when asked to lend a piece of broken tile or earthen plate on which to carry the embers, refuses to do so.

53. उज्यांत तेल. Putting oil into the fire. Adding insult to injury. आगींत तेल ओतणें. दीप्तालय विझवाया दादुनि घालील कोण तेलातें. (मोरोपंत, उद्योगपर्व)

54. उड्डा तो बुड्डा. The one who jumps high, falls down. Pride goes before a fall. चढेल तो पडेल आणि पोहेल तो बुडेल.

55. उण्याक वाट सुण्याक फाट. Do not interfere with a mean man, and walk away from a dog. Do not associate with mean men.

56. उदकाच्या बळार सुंगट उड्डा. The shrimp jumps up because it has the backing of water. A man spurns others because he has riches. Cf. आईजन्चिया जिवावर बाईजी उदार.

57. उदकांतली मांडकी उदक पियेल्याबगर रावता ! A frog living in water cannot but enjoy some of that water—This is in reference to the dishonesty of a man entrusted with money etc. तळें राखी तो पाणी चाखी.

58. उदाराचें पोतें सवायहात रितें. A man who buys on credit, has always an empty sack. उधाराचें पोतें सवा हात रितें.

59. उदक्कांतुलो कोब्बु.

(उदकांतलो कब्बू-उंस)

The sugar-cane standing in water. Sugar-cane that grows in the water is stout, long and beautiful to look at; but it has not got the natural sweetness and juice which one finds in a sugar-cane grown elsewhere. This proverb means grand outwardly and nasty inside. Cf. देखनेमें डब्बू और चलनेमें शिवराई.

60. उद्दारीची पोणु थू करप.

(उदारीच पडून थू करप)

To spit while lying on one's back; when he does that the spitting falls on his own body. To bring misfortunes on oneself by one's own actions.

61. उधकापस्सी पात्तळ करप.

(उधकापरस पातळ करप)

To make thinner than water. This is impossible. Any substance if added to water, is bound to make it thicker; so, the proverb is used when we want to make much of anything.

62. उधकारी माल्ल्यारी दोनीं जत्त वे ?
(उदकार माल्ल्यार दोन जातात व्हैय ?)

If one strikes on the surface of water does it break into two ? It is impossible to divide water by striking it with a stick.

63. उबो आसं मेरेन लाखाचो, मरतकूच फुकाचो. As long as the man is alive he is worth a lakh of rupees ; no sooner he dies, his worth is nothing.

64. *उमथी कोळश्यारी उधाक रकंवप.
(उमथ्या कळशार उदक रकीप)

Pouring water over a pot with its mouth turned downwards; which means that not a drop will enter the pot; a man who does so, loses his energy without doing good to anybody.

65. उमथी जालारींय नाक्क उधारी.
(उमथी जाल्यारूप नाख उदारें)

Even when she falls down on her belly with her face touching the ground, she boldly states that her nose was on the upperside, meaning that her nose did not touch the ground at all. Touching the ground with the nose is considered a sort of humiliation. Cf. Goldsmith's "Even though vanquished he would argue still."

66. उमथ्या कळशार उदक. Throwing water on the bottom of a pot turned upside down. It is no use teaching or advising a man who has not the receptivity for such teaching and advice. उपड्या घागरीवर पाणी. Cf. Prove. No. 64.

67. उमळपाक पाड आनी जेंवक वाड. Cannot wash clothes but wants free meals. The lazy man wants to enjoy at other's expense.

68. उलौंक कळना जाल्यार तोंड धांपचें. If you cannot talk, shut up your mouth. Do not try to show your wisdom when really you lack sense. Silence is golden when one does not know how to speak. Cf. मौनं सर्वार्थसाधनम्.

69. उश्टे हत्तान कैळाक आंबुडतल्लो.
(उश्ट्या हातान कावळ्याक आमुडतलो)

One who drives away crows by the hand by which he has taken his meals. The Hindus dine with their bare fingers; naturally some of the food sticks to their hand; if crows are driven away by that hand some of the food particles will fall down and the crows instead of going away will come nearer in the hope of picking them up. This means that the man really attracts those crows in an indirect way instead of driving them away. This really means that he does good by intending to do harm. A blessing in disguise. This proverb should be compared with the next No. 70.

70. उश्ट्या हातान कावळो आमडिना. A man does not like to drive away a crow, when his hand is full of food particles, being afraid that one of the food grains might fall down and so lost to himself. This is in reference to the most selfish man who never does an act of charity. तो उष्टया हातानें कावळा देखील हांकणार नाहीं. See prov. No. 69.

71. उश्णीं वायनां. Returning the presents received on some ceremonial occasions.

72. उश्णें दिवन दुबळो भिकारी जालो; उतर दिवन लखपति भिकारी जालो. A poor man is reduced to beggary by lending and a rich man by promising. The poor should not lend and the rich should not promise recklessly, because a promise has always to be kept.

73. एक दिस मांयलो, एक दिस सुनेलो. One day the mother-in-law is in power, and another day the daughter-in-law holds the

strings. Every dog has his day. चार दिवस सासूचे, चार दिवस सुनेचे. Cf. Pro. No. 80.

74. एक म्हज कालूं खैंचे तपलेंत घालूं ? I have only one oyster; where shall I keep it ? Some think too much and too highly of their own possessions. Say an only son in old age.

75. एक लेंड्या दोन कुडके, एक घाणटा आनी एक परमळटा ? Two portions or pieces taken out of the same excreta. Does one piece smell bad and the other sweet ? There is no choice in similar evils.

76. एकल्याचें चौगांनीं जेंव येत, पुण चौगांचें एकल्याच्यान जेंव नजे. Four persons can eat and digest one man's food, but one cannot eat and digest four persons' food.

77. एकल्यान बैल माल्ल्यार दुसऱ्यान गाय मारची न्हंय. If one has killed a bull, it does not mean that another should kill a cow. Because one man has done a wrong, another need not retaliate. एकानें गाय मारली म्हणून दुसऱ्यानें वांसरूं मारूं नये. Cf. Pro. No. 150.

78. एकादसीगेर शिवरात. Ekadashi and Shivratri are both religious days of observing a fast; when Shivratri is the guest of Ekadashi there is nothing but complete starvation. A beggar cannot expect anything from another beggar. एकादशीचे घरीं शिवरात्र. Cf. Pro. No. 388.

79. एका फारान सतरा वाग. Killing 17 tigers at one shot. Exaggerating one's own powers. Bragging too much.

80. एकु काळु मार्यीचो जालारी एकु काळु सुनेचो.
(एक काळ मांयचो जाल्यार एक काळ सुनेचो)

If the mother-in-law exerts authority at one time, the day will arrive when the daughter-in-law will be in full power. Every dog has his day. Cf. Pro. No. 73.

81. ओज्यार बिंजें.
(ओज्यार अवखादो)

Adding weight to a burden i.e., increasing hardships. Misfortunes never come single. इयं गंडस्योपरि पिटिका संवृत्ता। A pimple has grown upon a boil. अभाळावर अभाळ येणें. Cf. Prov. No. 116.

82. ओडी वाइटी मोणु दक्टिी केली ; तिज्जे पय्याक तीनी.
(व्हडली वायट म्हुण धाकटी केली ; तिच्या पांयाक तीन)

Seeing that the first wife was bad, one married a second wife but she was worse. Literally her legs have three faults. Old things even though they are bad, are better than new things which appear good.

83. ओल्ले शेणा उज्जो लघल्यावरी.
(ओल्या शेणाक उजो लागल्यावरी)

Like the fresh cow-dung catching fire Cow-dung is dried and burnt to get ashes which are used by the Shaivites to annoint their bodies with. When the cow-dung is dry it burns very easily ; when it is fresh it takes much more time to burn and even then it burns very very slowly. So, when anybody is doing any work slowly and without any intelligence, we say that he is just like a man trying to burn fresh cow-dung.

84. कणकींतसून काड, भोबो नाका. I do not want any sweets; but do get me out of the Bambu clump. Get me out of my difficulties. भीक नको पण कुत्रा आवर.

85. कपलांतु नात्तिल्लाक कोंकुनु गाल्लारी वोक्कुनु वत्ता.
(कपळांत नाथिल्ल्याक कोंकून घाल्यार ओंकून वेता)

A thing which is not written in the forehead of a man by Fate, falls out when forcibly injected there. Even if it be put in there it is vomited out. This proverb is based on the belief of "Shirolikhitam" (kismet) and is used when some misfortune falls on anybody, in spite of fortunate surroundings. It is "so destined" is the verdict.

86. कयीळो नव्हारी डोंक जत्ता वे ?
(कावळो न्हाल्यार डॉक जाता व्हय ?)

If a crow bathes will it become a crane? The crow is black and the crane is white. A wicked man will never become virtuous.

87. कर्यांतु उधाक मुंग्येक समुद्रु.
(कर्टेतलें उदक मुयेक समुद्र)

Water in a cocoanut shell is a sea to an ant. A little wealth is considered a great riches by a poor person.

88. करिनाशिल्ल्यान केल्यार जायनाशिलें जाता. One who has never done anything, tries to do something, the impossible happens *i.e.*, he succeeds.

89. कवडेंतु हाणु कोळसो बेत्तप.
(कवर्डेत हाडून कळसो फोडप)

To break the pot of water after having brought it upto the gate. By carrying the pot of water from the village well which is generally at a great distance upto the gate of the house and then to break it accidentally there at the gate is to make all the previous labour useless and futile. When anybody does hard work to the end and the whole trouble ends in a smoke we use this proverb.

90. कळ्ळांतुलो पेट्ट.
(काळखांतलो पेट)

Blows received in the dark.

91. काजुलो — केलदें — आपलेच्च गांडीक तोखेता. The fire (glow) worm is always charmed of his own buttocks. Petty people always consider themselves to be the wisest or richest etc. Applauding oneself above others. माकड म्हणतें आपलीच गांड लाल.

92. कातरल्यारी मीठ घालुनतिलो.
(कातल्स्यार मीठ घाल्निनाशिलो.)

One who would not apply salt to another's wound. This means a man who is cruel-hearted and will not be of any use to anybody.

93. कान खाता तें भांगर कानांत घाल्चें न्हंय. One should not use a gold ornament if that ornament eats up the ear itself. However valuable and tempting a thing or a person may be, if that be not conducive to one's interests or does not remain grateful, it should be shunned. Cf. विद्या समन्वितहि दुष्ट परि त्यजावा । त्यासीं बुधें न सहवास कधीं करावा ॥ Also खाल्ल्या घरचे वांसे मोजणारा. An ungrateful person tries to injure his benefactor, however kindly he may be treated. Cf. फणी दुग्धातेंही पिउनि गरळातेंच वमती ।

94. कान दोळे सुज्जौन सव्यार सुंट फुल्ल्या. Dry ginger is grown on stony grounds and has blossomed now after giving intense pain to eyes and ears. This is in respect of the success one obtains amidst tremendous difficulties and after undergoing all sorts of hardships. Cf. मुसळाला अंकूर फुटणें.

95. कान फूक म्हळ्यार वायन फुकता. When asked to blow soothing breath in the ear, he blows breath in the grain-pounding-hole. Doing the wrong thing. डोळ्यांत केर आणि कानांत फुंकर.

96. काप गेले दोते उल्ले. The earrings have gone leaving behind big holes in the lobes of the ears. This means that while prosperity is lost, the delapidated marks of past affluence, which are often an eyesore, are left. Cf. Pro. No. 198.

97. कापणी करून वार विचारता. Why ask the day after the shave? It is customary among orthodox Hindus to have a shave on particular days of the week and also on special days of the lunar month. It is no use inquiring which occasion

would be the most suited to do a thing after the thing is actually done. कन्या देऊनियां कुळ मग काय विचारावें !

98. काम करतल्याची फाट आनी जेवतल्याचें तोंड पळों नाका. Do not look at the back of a labourer when working and at the mouth of a person who is dining. Both look ugly.

99. काम जालें, वैज मेलो. The work is over and the Doctor is dead; *i.e.*, nobody cares for the Doctor when the patient is alright. There is in-gratitude in this world. गरज सरो वैद्य मरो. कामापुरता मामा, ताका पुरती आजीबाई.

100. कामा चोर मुशाऱ्या हजर Would not work, but is present at the time of paying wages. Those that do not labour are however ready to take credit. कामाला मागें व तोबऱ्याला पुढें.

101. कामीणकाराक सगळेंच हळ्डुवें A man attacked with jaundice, sees all things yellow. A prejudiced man cannot see things rightly. कावीळ झालेल्यास जग पिंवळें.

102. कावळो बसूंक आनी ताळी मोडूंक एक जालें. The crow sits on the branch and the branch breaks at the same time by chance Sometimes things happen so simultaneously that we consider one is the result of another. काकतालीय न्याय.

103. कावळ्या-दोळो तवश्या-पिगरेर (निडयेर) The crow always has an eye on the tender cucumber. Some people have an eye always to their gain and look out for an opportunity चोरांचें लक्ष गांठोड्यावर.

104. कासु दिवनु लासु घेवप. To buy calamity by paying cash To undergo unnecessary hardships.

105. कांट्यान कांटो काडचो. Remove a thorn by using a thorn itself. शठं प्रति शाठ्यम्.

धटासी आणावा धट । उद्धटासी पाहिजे उद्धट ।
खटनटासी खटनट । अगत्य करी ॥

दासबोध. १९-९-३०.

106. कांय केल्यार कांय आसं, न्याय केल्यार अर्दे आसं. If you do something you get something. If you fight in a court, you have the chance of getting at least a half ? There is nothing like a trial. (The Konkan Districts are notorious for litigation.)

107. किर्पिणाक दुपेट खर्चे. A miser has to spend twice as much. Penny-wise and pound-foolish. लोभ्या दुणा खर्च.

108. किंर्गळें बोट सुजल्यार कितलें सुजत ? If the little finger of the hand swells, it cannot swell too much and get too thick: There is a limit to everything. करंगळी सुजली म्हणून डोंगरा एवढी होईल काय ?

109. कुड्डो मागता एक दोळो, देवान ताका दोन दिले. The blind man prays for one eye and God gives him two. Sometimes our wishes are fulfilled beyond expectation. आंधळा मागतो एकच डोळा, देव देतो दोन.

110. कुड्डयाक चाळीसपत्र किल्याक ? A blind man needs no spectacles. A man who has no sense, cannot be wiser by advice. वांझेस कातबोळ.

111. कुणब्या हातांत जवाद दिली, आंबिली वांगडा भाजून खाली. If you give sweet-scented musk to a boor, he will fry it and eat it with his gruel. You cannot expect ignorant fools to make right use of things however valuable they may be. गाढवापुढें वाचिली गीता, कालचा गोंधळ बरा होता. गाढवास गुळाची चव काय?

112. कुड्ड्यांक काणसो रायु.
(कुड्डयांक काणो राया)

One-eyed is a king to the blind. आंधोबांत कान्होबा राजा

113. कुड्ड्यां हातांतुलो दिवो.
(कुड्डया हातांतलो दिवो.)

A lamp in the hands of a blind man. This is of no use to him.

114. कुराड घेवन गेल्लो राना, किर्तें हाडलें म्हळ्यार कांय ना. He went to the jungles with the hatchet (to bring wood) but brought nothing. Some put on showy appearances and brag about their abilities, but actually they do nothing.

115. कुल्याचें सोडून माथ्याक रेवडायता. Take off the loin-cloth and cover up the head. Exposing one's frailties and subjecting oneself to ridicule. ढुंगणाचें सोडून डोक्यास गुंडाळणें.

116. कुशिल्ल्यांत सुणें हागलें. The dog has passed stools in a rotten article. A bad thing rendered worse. Cf. ओज्यार बिजें. Prov. No. 81.

117. कुस्सल्ल्या शिताक करपल्ली ओटी.
(कुशिल्ल्या शिताक करपलें ओंट)

For the putrid rice a burnt *oti*. Oti is the dried rind of a fruit having acid taste; it is used in making sour sauce. Birds of the same feather. Cf. लास्सल्ल मासळेक कुस्सल्ली चिंच. (No. 462).

118. कुळारी थायकिळी किर्लेली.
(कुळारा तायाखिळो किल्लो)

Weeds have grown up in the place where the family house was situated. This means that the family had become extremely poor having lost all their property, house etc.

119. कुंडो खातल्याक उंडयाची रूच किर्ते ? A man who lives on chaff cannot appreciate the taste of bread. You should cultivate a taste of things if you really want to enjoy them.

120. कुंभकर्णाली सेवा. The worship of कुंभकर्ण. It is said that कुंभकर्ण worshipped sleep; for he slept for six months continuously. This is in reference to one who is overfond of sleep.

121. कुंभाराक मडकी धंड ना. The potter has no sound pot for his own use. Those who spend their life's energy in the

service of others, have no pleasures themselves. Cf. वैद्याचीं भुरगीं मुयांनीं खालीं. कुंभारास मडकें धड नाहीं. पगडबंदाचें पागोटें मोडकें. चांभाराचा जोडा फाटका. वैद्याचीं पोरें गालगुंडानें मेलीं.

122. कुंभाराची मडकी सदींच फुटकी. The potter's pot is always broken. Cf. कुंभाराक मडकी धड ना. See above proverb.

123. केल्लीं कर्मां ह्याच जल्मां. We have to suffer and reap the fruit of our actions (sins) in this very life. Reap as you sow. दळील तो भरील. ह्या हातानें करावें व त्या हातानें भरावें. कलजुग नहीं, करजुग है. इस हातसे दे, उस हातसे ले.

124. कोणाच्या व्हराडा कोण मुरडा ? Why take trouble for others with whom we are not concerned ? Cf. कोणाच्यो म्हशी, कोण काट्टा उठाबशी. गांवांत ह्माळ, सुण्याक बोवाळ. See the proverb below.

125. कोणाच्यो म्हशी, कोण काट्टा उठाबशी. The buffaloes belong to others and one who is not their owner is anxious for them. Why care for concerns which do not concern you ? Cf. Pro. No. 158.

126. कोलो ऊंशेलांत पडलो. Like the fox in the sugar-cane plantation. Happy in the best circumstances so much so that he does not know what to do. त्याला घबाड साधलें.

127. कोल्याक शिदाव फारीग करचो लागना. The fox has not to pay the tax.

128. कोंकण्यांल्या भटापाश्ट. Worse than a Hindu priest. Here Konkano means a gentile. It is a Christian proverb.

129. कोंबो गेलो तारवार, कोंबी जाली गुरवार. The cock has gone on a voyage and the hen has become pregnant. This shows infidelity.

130. कोंब्याच्या बळार कोंबी उट्टा, घोवाच्या बळार बायल उट्टा. Owing to the help of the cock, the hen is proud and undaunting,

just as the wife is, because of her husband's support. The weak derive support by their alliance with the strong. Cf. अंगणांतला कुत्रा. नक्रः स्वस्थानमासाद्य गजेंद्रमपि कर्षति ।

131. खज्जुरु पिकल्ल वेळेरी कयीळाक तोण्णांतु रुंव.
(खाजूर पिकिल्ल्या वेळार कावळ्या–तोंडांत रुं.)

When the dates are ripe, the crow's mouth gets sore. This is used when a man is unable to take advantage of the good fortune that is waiting foi him.

132. खळ्य–उंचय नात्तिल्लो.
(खालाय–उंचाय नाथिल्लो)

One who has neither the bottom nor the top. A man of straw. Cf. मूळ्य वळ्ळीय नात्तिल्लो (No. 427).

133. खंद्यारी बेस्सुनु कानु खावप.
(खांधार बसून कान खावप)

To bite at the ear while sitting on the shoulder. Pretending to be a sincere friend and working to ruin him.

134. खाडाक उज्जो लाघल वेळेरी अपलो बज्जूंक वत्ता.
(खाडाक उजो लागल्या वेळार अपलो भाजूंक वेता)

When another's beard is on fire, one bakes his *aplo* (bread) on it. When a person is in danger another tries to snatch some benefit out of it. *Aplo* is a kind of preparation made of black gram, salt, etc.

135. खाणा वेळेरी मेणा–दोळे, खेळीच्या वेळेरी मनुष्य दोळे.
(खाणा–वेळार मेणा–दोळे, खेळा–वेळार मनशा–दोळे)

Turning the eyes as soft as wax at the time of eating and making them hard when asked to play (work ?). This means that a man tries to attract compassion when asking for a favour ; but he puts on quite a different expression when he is asked to pay back that obligation.

136. खात्याक आस्ता भोव, न्हात्याक चिखोल भोव. The more you eat, the more your appetite is kindled. The more you wash, the more you become dirty. Those who are not content, get more and more worried. Cf. the next proverb.

137. खायत तितली भूक भोव, न्हायत तितलो म्हेळ भोव. The more you eat the more you are hungry. The more you bathe the more you are dirty. Cf. the proverb above.

138. खारव्यांक गोरवां, शिद्द्यांक तारवां. A fisherman cannot tend cattle nor can the negro navigate ships. You cannot expect all people to do all things. जेनूं कांम ते करे; बाकी बीजा फांफां मारे. जेनूं काम तेनूं थाय; बीजा करे ते गोता खाय. वेड्याचें बागडें व सुताराचें तागडें. Cf. Pro. No. 149.

139. खांकून खांकून गांवकार जाता. The headman of a village has a peculiar way of coughing and asserting his superiority. The proverb means—You have become a village headman by coughing. Rising to a post without real merit but by pretensions. लब्धप्रातिष्ठित.

140. खांडयेक एकवीस कुडव पोल. The *Khandy* has twenty one bushels useless grain or seed. (The khandy consists of twenty bushels). There is not a grain of truth in the statement. It is full of lies. मूठभर मिया हातभर दाढी. आठ हात लांकूड नऊ हात ढलपी.

141. खांवक–जेंवक आसल्यार सोयरे खूब. If you have plenty to eat you get many relatives about you. Opulence brings many friends while poverty drives them away. असतील शितें तर मिळतील भुतें. शितें जोंवरी भुतें भोंवतीं । कोण कुणाचा सखा जिवा ।

142. खांवचें घोवाचें आनी घेंवचें मिंडाचें ? To live on the labours of one's husband and to receive taunts from the paramour. Cf. कसायाला गाय धारजिणी.

143. खुंठु नत्तिले वोयी मंधप.
(खुंट नाशिली वैय बांदप)

To make a fence without using posts. For putting up a fence, the most necessary things are the upright posts ; if they be absent the fence will not stand up. This would mean to do a thing without doing the most important and necessary part of it.

144. खैं गा वेता ? खोरजुव्यां ; म्हजेंय खोरजुलें. It is a pun on the word. Where are you going ? To Khorzuvem (an island in Goa). The other man answers, I have also got an itching to go to Khorzuvem.

145. खैं गेल्लो ? खैं ना ; कितें हाडलें ? कांय ना. Where had you gone ? Nowhere. What have you brought ? Nothing. There are some who aimlessly do things and get nothing. A sort of rolling stone. Cf. बारा पिंपळांवरचा मुंजा.

146. खोबऱ्याचो बैल चलता बरो. The bullock laden with dry copra walks well ; for, it expects to have a share of that copra. Cf. को न याति वशं लोके मुखं पिंडेन पूरितः । मृदंगो मुखलेपेन करोति मधुरध्वनिम् ।

147. खोरें आपलेवशीन माती ओढ्टा. The hoe is drawn to one's own side. You are always partial to yourself and to your own side. आपल्या पोळीवर तूप ओढणें. खोरें आपल्याकडेसच माती ओढतें.

148. गरजवंताक अक्कल ना. A needy man has no sense. The needy are indiscreet. गरजवंताला अक्कल नसते. Cf. अडला नारायण गाढवाचे पाय धरी.

149. गाबत्या गोरूं, भटा तारूं. The fisherman is unfit to tend cattle and the priest to navigate a ship. Cf. खारव्यांक गोरवां शिङ्यांक तारवां. Prov. No. 138.

150. गायिक मारली मोणु वांसराक मारत्ताती वे ?
(गायक माल्ली म्हूण वांसराक मारतात न्हय ?)

Because one killed a cow, is it right for another to kill the calf ? Cf. Pro. No. 77.

151. गायिक विंवुचो वेळु; पाड्याक तिक्का बायल कोरचो वेळु.
(गायचो वियेंवचो वेळ; पाड्याक तिका बायल करचो वेळ)

For a cow it is the time of her delivery; whereas for the bullock it is the time to make her his wife. While the cow is suffering from the confinement pains, the bullock wants to enjoy her society without paying the least heed to her condition. This is in reference to extreme selfishness of some persons.

152. गायिचें चाम गाल्लोलो वागु.
(गायचें चाम घाल्लो वाग)

A tiger wearing the hide of a cow. Cf. The wolf in lamb's clothing.

153. गांड धुवन कडी करता. A very miserly man. Cf. Prov. No. 436.

154. गांडीक ना फाळी, गांड मागता कायलोळी. The buttocks are not even covered by rags, but the woman longs for sweet cakes. बरावर नाहीं कौल आणि रिकामा डौल.

155. गांडीक पडलो घाव, वैज जाल्लो मांव. There is a wound at the private part and the father-in-law is the doctor to whom it has to be shown. Sometimes you have to give out secrets to those from whom you have to hide them. नाजुक ठिकाणीं (अडचणींत) रोग आणि जांवई वैद्य.

156. गांडीक शेण लावन बैल जाता. Jack-daw in the peacock's feather. शेण लावा आणि बैल म्हणा.

157. गांडींत घर करून पादाक अळशीकचें न्हय. If you have made a house in the buttocks, you cannot call dung dirty. When you

have chosen to live amidst dirty environments, you have to put up with them. Cf. पाण्यांत राहून माशाशीं वैर.

158. गांवांत ह्माळ, सुण्याक बोवाळ. There are feasts in the village in commemoration of the dead and the dog is very busy. Sometimes persons who have no concern, unnecessarily busy themselves though nobody cares for them, perhaps like the dog to gain some end. Cf. Pro. No. 125. गांवांत ह्माळ व कुत्र्यास बोवाळ.

159. गांवा सारको भेस गुरू सारको उपदेस. Dress yourself according to the fashion of the country and expect advice from the preceptor according to his capacity. Adapt yourself to the condition in which you are placed without expecting to do or to have too much. When you go to Rome, do as Rome does. देश तसा वेश.

160. गिरेस्तांलो वाडो, न्हेसूंक मेळना फाडो. What is the use of a mansion when one does not get a rag even to put on ?

161. गुरुत्वं नात्तिल्ल्याक तिन्नीयकडे.
(गुरुत्व नाथिल्ल्याक तिनीयकडेन)

One who has not got the grace or the blessings of his *Guru* (preceptor) but on the contrary has incurred his curse, loses at three places *i.e.*, everywhere.

162. गुळेर दिवनुं वांयगण घेवप.
(गुळेर दिवन वांयगें घेवप)

To receive a big brinjal in return for a small superior sort of fruit like brinjal. To exchange a horse for an ass. Cf. Prov. No. 36.

163. गोड ना जाल्यार गोडासारकें उतर ना ? If you cannot give molasses, can't you at least speak sweetly ? You do not lose anything by a sweet tongue. गुळ नाहीं पण गुळाची वाचा तरी असावी.

164. गॉयांत व्हडीं, घाटार घोडीं. There are small boats in Goa and ponies on the Ghats (hills). You cannot use boats on the Ghats and horses in Goa which is a group of islands. Every country has its own articles of use.

165. गोवंटेच्या सवंतणेन जीब आस्सील्लो.
(गोमटे भोंवतणी जीब आशिल्लो)

One who has got a tongue all round the neck. A prattler or wayward in speech.

166. घर अस्कड, बायल माकड त्या दादल्याक ना सांकड. If the house be uninhabitable or desolate and the wife ugly like the monkey, the husband has no fear of his losing either the house or the wife. घर सांकड आणि बाईल माकड.

167. घरचो चोर जिवानशीं मारता. A thief of your acquaintance kills you outright so that his identity may not be out. Those who know you best, often prove to be your worst enemies. ओळखीचा चोर जिवानिशीं मारतो.

168. घर-मोगऱ्याक पोमोंळ ना.
(घर-मोगऱ्याक पर्मळ ना)

The sweet-scented jasmine flowers in front of the house have no fragrance. Too much familiarity breeds contempt. A prophet is no prophet in his own land.

169. घर मोडून मांटव. Dismantle a house and put up a mandap with the materials. Destroying good things and going in for useless ones or to take useless things in exchange for those that are really valuable. Cf. Selling his birth right for a mess of pottage.

170. घरांतली कथा, पोटांतली व्यथा, कोणा सांगून येना. Family secrets as well as pain in the abdomen cannot be understood by others, or cannot be told to others.

171. घरांत हुंदीर शेंपड्यो बडैतात. The mice thrash their tails on the floor, because they do not get anything to eat. This shows extreme poverty. चुलिमध्यें मांजर व्याली आहे. चुलीस अक्षद लागली आहे.

172. घालता जाल्यार घालगे रांडे भीक, हांव पेडणेंचो भिकारी. The insolent beggar asks for charity in an offensive tone, as he comes from Pedne, a place noted for its cheekiness.

173. चलतल्याची चाल कळटा, उलैतल्याचें उतर कळटा. You can know the speed of a man from his walk and the wisdom of a man from his talk. You can judge the things from observation.

174. चली दिवची मोटयागेर आनी सून हाडची गरिबाली. Give your daughter in marriage into a rich family, but get a daughter-in-law from a poor one. मुलगी द्यावी श्रीमंताकडे पण करावी गरिबाची.

175. चाखरी केल्यार भाकरी आसं. Serve and you get bread. Laziness won't pay. राबेल तो चाबील. खटपट करी तो पोट भरी.

176. चामडी दीत पुण दमडी दिना. He would rather give the skin of his body, but not a pie. That shows a nature too stingy. चामडी देईल पण दमडी देणार नाहीं

177. चाम्हाराचो आंड कसो भोंवता. He wanders like the balls of a shoe-maker. He wanders aimlessly.

178. चाम्हारा देवाक जोत्या-पुजा. The shoemaker's God should be worshipped not with flowers but with shoes. Give what one deserves. चांभाराच्या देवास खेटराची पुजा.

179. चुकिलें गोरूं धामापुरच्या तळ्यांत. There is a tank in the village of Dhamapur where stray cattle is to be found. This is in reference to hospitality. There are certain families noted for their hospitality and when a stranger enters a village he finds a ready welcome there. Dhamapur is a village in the county of Salsete in Goa.

180. चुकीक दोळे नात. Mistake has no eyes. Those that commit mistakes, do so accidentally.

181. चुहृेवो सोरोप. Taking the rope for a serpent. Anticipating danger where there is none. रज्जु-सर्प न्याय. दोरीच्या सापा भिउनि भवा, भेट नाहीं शिवा शिवा ।

182. चून कांतून आनी उतर चितून पळोंचें. Scratch out the kernel from the cocoanut and you know the quality of the fruit; also ponder over the words and you know a wise man. If you want to taste a man listen to his answers as you do in the case of a cocoanut by scratching out a little kernel. भाताची परीक्षा शितावर.

183. चेडी मंथारी जाल्लारी पतिव्रता जत्ता !
(चेडी म्हातारी जाल्यार पतिव्रता जाता !)

Can a harlot be called a chaste woman when she becomes aged ? *Chedis* are a sect of people living in Cochin and Travancore speaking Konkani language. They are sometimes called Deva-dasis. They are connected with dancing etc., in the temples of the Gaud Sarasvat community.

184. चेडो माडावरी, चेडूं केळीवरी. The boy like the cocoapalm and the girl like the plantain tree. The bridegroom strong and healthy and the bride tender and sweet, make a good match.

185. चेल्ली चिन्हा, दोळे कुडें.
(चली सुंदर, दोळे कुड्डे)

The girl is handsome but her eyes are blind. Everything is excellent except the one thing most needed.

186. चोर उठून कोतवालाक धरता. The thief catches the head of the police. Thrusting blame on the innocent. Cf. चोर तो चोर आणि पुन्हा शिरजोर.

187. चोर चोराक गवाय. Thief standing as a surety to another thief. You cannot trust those who are not trustworthy.

188. चोराक चांदन्याचो हुस्को. The thief is anxious about the coming of moonlight. Those who have dark intentions, avoid publicity.

189. चोराच्या भयान घेतलें रान, थैं मेळ्ळो मुसलमान, ताणें कापले नाख-कान. A man ran to the jungle to avoid the thief. There a Musalman caught him and cut off his nose and ears. If you try to avoid one danger you are sometimes landed into greater dangers. The same proverb is to be found in Marathi.

190. चोरा–मनांत चांदनें. The thief thinks, there is moonlight when really there is none. The guilty has no clear conscience.

191. चोरा–शिनळाक तोंड भोव. The thief and the adulterous persons put up a strong defence. The offenders are the first to pretend innocence.

192. चोरांची आवै हड्डुयांत रड़ा. A thief's mother weeps secretly, because if she should weep openly, her son would be caught. When your secret plans fail, you cannot have the sympathy of any man nor there is anybody to guide you.

193. चोरी करची आपल्या गांवांत, भीक मागची दुसऱ्याच्या गांवांत. A man may commit a theft in his own village. His local knowledge helps him. But he should beg in another village where nobody knows who he is.

194. जसो रूख तशें फळ. Just as the tree, so is the seed. जसा वृक्ष तसें फळ. खाण तशी माती. यथा बीजं तथांकुरः Cf. Pro. No. 367.

195. जळव्या घरा कोलू. To take the unburnt grass from the grass-thatch of a burning house. Make the most of what you can get, however little it may be. जळत्या घराचा बळता (पोळता) वांसा. चोराची लंगोटी.

196. जळे रे कोंड्या जळेता, गुवांत तकली लोळेता. A man gets annoyed unnecessarily and puts his head in a dung-hill.

197. जंगो दक्षोवनु फले करप.
(जांगो दाखौन फालें करप)

To engage a paramour for the whole night and to send him away disappointed at dawn by showing him only the thighs. Literally it means "to make it dawn by showing only the thighs." This proverb has a vulgar origin, but it is in common use when people want to get out of their promises by artful and tricky means.

198. जंद्यो गेल्यो खिणां उर्ली. The chainlike ornament in the foot is gone but the marks are left. Opulence is gone but the marks of opulence are still there. काप गेले व भोंकें राहिलीं. Cf. Prov. No. 96.

199. जाचें कुडें ताचे फुडें. Curses like chickens come home to roost. Evil to him who evil thinks. ज्याचें कुडें त्यापुढें.

200. जाचें मन भोळें ताका देव दिता केळें; जाचें मन कपट ताका देव दिता थापट. A simpleton will get a plantain and a crafty man will get a blow from God. In this world the simple and frank person succeeds better than the crafty man. Cf. मन चंगा तो काठोटीमे गंगा.

201. जाती कोंकोणो कर्म नस्ताणी.
(जात कोंकणी कर्म नस्ताणी)

Konkani by caste, but Christian by acts. Naturally the Goan Christians are looked down upon by the Konkani people; so when a Hindu does something dirty he is called a Christian.

202. जाल्ल्या–सभाव मेल्याबगर वचना. The habit sticks on until you die. Habit is second nature. जित्याची खोड मेल्यावांचून जात नाहीं.

203. जांगेपरस लंवयड मोटें. The muscle is larger or bigger than the thigh and not in proportion to it. If you have servants who want to rule over you, surely they are dangerous. Cf. नाकापेक्षां मोतीं जड.

204. जिवानशीं मरतल्याक केंशीं सोडलो. The man was allowed to go home safe, who was destined to die, after simply depriving him of his hair. जिवावर आलें होतें तें शेपटीवर गेलें.

205. जीब नत्तिल्लो केप्याक कीरु करता.
(जीब नाथिल्लो भेन्याक कीर करता.)

A dumb man makes fun of a deaf man. Although one is in want of an important organ like the tongue he does not hesitate to make fun of another who has lost his hearing.

206. जीव वचना म्हुण हात-पांय बडैता. He struggles because his life does not become extinct. Struggling to the last without hope of success.

207. जेविल्ल्या घराचे वांसे मेजता. Counting the bamboos of the roof of a house under which you are fed with food (with a view to buy the house etc.) Turning ungrateful. खाल्ल्या घरचे वांसे मोजणारा. See below.

208. जेविल्ल्या पानार हागता. Making stools on the leaf on which you are fed. Turning ungrateful. खातो तेथें हगतो. See above.

209. जें फूल माळना तें फूल हुंगना. Indian ladies do not smell the flowers which they do not want to wear in the head. Do not worry yourself with things that do not concern you. Cf. गमन नसे ज्या गांवीं, तेथील वाट कशास पुसावी।

210. जेंवक ना जाल्यार गोठ्यांत वाड. If you have no food to give me please feed me in the cow-pen. The question is not of finding out where to feed, but what to feed with.

211. जेवक नाशिल्ल्याक उश्या—अळशीक? A man who has no food to eat, should not reject leavings of food. You have to be satisfied with a little when you can not get as much as you require. मांडा नाहीं तर कोंडा.

212. जो उदकांत देंवना तो व्हाण काडिना. The one who does not go into the water, need not take off the shoes. Only those who enter a venturesome business, have to forego their own pleasure. Cf. श्रमाविण फळ नाहीं.

213. जोर रहा खैं पेजेक, बैरंव रहा खैं जागेक. The fever was starved out of a poor man who had nothing to eat. The cob-web had also to remain out because there was no suitable place for it. See preface.

214. झगड्याक बळ कसलें? उत्तर येतां तसलें. What feeds a quarrel? It is the exchange of words which inflames a quarrel. Quarrels will not stop as long as the two parties do not shut up. Compare the story of पदरांत विस्तव

215. झड वारें येता आसताना माडा—मुळांत रांवचें न्हय. When there is a strong wind blowing, do not stand under a cocoanut tree, lest the nuts should fall and smash your head. Whenever there is a dangerous movement going on, try to avoid it.

216. णोय आंडाक चोय. When one is ninety, he is too much bowed down ; literally he looks at his balls.

217. तकली माल्ल्यार खोंकली गेली. Cut off the head and the cough will cease. You should not take extreme measures for petty matters. गळा कापला खोकला गेला.

218. तळव विस्सरनु तेल दवरप.
(ताळू विसरून तेल घालप.)

To smear oil on the head forgetting the centre of the head. There is a custom that for an oil bath, the oil must be first smeared at the centre of the head as it is the most important part of the body. A man who works against his community or society is said to be like a man who smears oil on any other part of the body first, other than the centre of the head.

219. तळें राखतलो उदकाक मरना. A man who preserves a tank will not be in want of water. Those that make provision for bad times are happy. आपदर्थे धनं रक्षेत् । Cf. Prov. No. 451.

220. ताक माडा–मुळांत व्हरून सूर म्हुण पियेता. He drinks buttermilk under a cocoa palm so that people may think that he is drinking toddy. Question of stupid vanity. Cf. मिशांना तूप लावणें.

221. ताकाक येवन बुडकुलो लिपेता. You have come to take buttermilk and you hide the pot in which you are to take the buttermilk. False shame. ताकाला जाऊन भांडें लपविणें.

222. ताका फावना म्हाका रूण ना.

223. ताणें पांयांनीं गांठायलें हाच्यान हातांनीं सोडौं नजे. He cannot unloosen with his hands, what the other has tied with his leg. There are some whose ingenious plans cannot be unravelled notwithstanding better brain work.

224. तारी दुडु दिवनु पोवनु वचप. Having paid money for the ferry to cross the river, one is obliged to come across by swimming. Having paid the hotel charges, one has to go on an empty stomach.

225. तारूं भरूंक गेल्लो आयलो; पोट भरूंक गेल्लो यॆंवक ना. The men who had gone to load the ship with cargo have returned, but the sailors who have gone on the ship as servants have not returned. It is easier to fill in the ship than the belly.

226. तांतयांत आसताना साद घालता. The chicken crows while yet in the egg. There are some who want to assert their superiority and wisdom while yet in their teens. Cf. काल मेला आज पितर झाला.

227. तीन म्हैन्यांच्या खाणाक एका दिसाचो जोर पुरो. A man may feed himself for three months and get strong; but in one day he will lose all the strength when fever attacks him. Our accumulated wealth is wiped off within a moment when calamity befalls. तेली सांचवी धार धार, खुदा नेतो एकच वार.

228. तूप खाल्ल्यालें रूप समजता. We can know the face of a man who eats ghee, *i.e.*, when a man eats ghee his face and complexion become healthy. Thus you can know from the contented appearance that a man is well-to-do and prosperous etc.

229. तुपा–आशेर लेंडे गिळळे. Do not eat dung because it is immersed in ghee. People do wicked and dirty things for small gain. तुपासाठीं उष्टें खाणें.

230. तुस्सु कंडुनु हत्ताक फोडु काडप.
(तूस कांडून हाताक फोड काडप)
or (फोड काड्टा)

To get boils on one's palms by pounding husk. To undergo unnecessary trouble without any gain. तुषकंडण न्याय– पिष्टपेषण.

231. तेवशिन गेल्यार न्हंय, हेवशीन गेल्यार बांय. Go that way and there is a river, and come this way and there is a well. Sometimes whatever side we may turn to there is danger. A dilemma. Between the devil and the deep sea. इकडे आड तिकडे विहीर.

232. तेंकुडेन ह्मोंवु काडप.
(तेंकडेन ह्मोंव काडप)

To collect honey with a long pole. When persons try to do things by stupid means and fail, we use this proverb. Cf Prov. No. 522.

233. तेंडल्याक बियो चंड, मोटव्याक बुद्द चंड, The small fruit called तेंडलें has many seeds and a short man has more wisdom. Short men are generally supposed to be wise.

234. तोंड वांकडें म्हळ्यार हारसो वांकडो म्हणूं येत? If the face be ugly, the looking glass cannot be said to be ugly. You look as you are. Cf. नाचतां येत नाहीं, आंगण वांकडें.

235. तोंडान बरो, पोटांत विखाचो पोळो. Sweet in words but poison in the belly. There are persons who talk sweet but are dangerous. मधु तिष्ठति जिव्हाग्रे हृदये तु हलाहलम्. Cf. Pro. No. 237.

236. तोंडार मारचें, पुण पोटार मारचें न्हंय. Strike a man on the face but strike not on the belly. *i.e.* Never mind if you punish a man, but do not deprive a man of his bread. पाठीवर मार पण पोटावर मारूं नकोस. Cf. Pro. No. 344.

237. तोंडांत मोग काळजांत रोग. Loving words in the mouth but disease in the heart. Cf. Proverb No. 235.

238. तोंडांतु बोट गल्लारी चब्बुक कोलुनात्तिल्लो.
(तोंडांत बोट घाल्यार चावूंक कळनाशिल्लो)

One who does not know how to bite at a finger placed in his mouth. This means a very innocent person.

239. थळथळेंचें सग्ग भंगार नयी.
(लकलकता तें सगळेंच भांगर न्हंय)

All that glitters is not gold.

240. थंडेंत कांबळ जड कोणाक? Who feels the blanket heavy when there is cold, *i.e.*, you do not feel those troublesome who help you in your peril.

241. थोंटाचें कि भटाचें. Let it belong to anybody, either to a lame man or to a priest. I don't care. I must have it.

242. थोंटें-मोडकें कुशीचें, पोल-सोल शेताचें. One's own child however decrepit and lame is dear to one, just as the produce of one's own field is, however poor in quality it may be. आपला तो बाब्या.

243. दर्यांत आसे मासो, ताचें मोल करतलो पिसो. The man who ascertains the value of a fish while it is in the sea, is a fool. Only fools speculate and base hopes of profits on it. Cf. बाजारांत तुरी, भट भटणीला मारी. कशाला नाहीं ठिकाण आणि बुधवारचें लग्न. पाण्यांत म्हैस, बाहेर मोल करणें.

244. दादा ब्राह्मण होनी सवाशीण. One's own brother and sister-in-law to be treated as the persons to be fed at the religious feast. This shows how some people selfishly confine their charities and duties to their own kith and kin. दादा ब्राह्मण वहिनी सवाष्ण.

245. दान मेळल्ले गायिचे दांत चोवप आस्स वे ?
(दान मेळिल्ले गायचे दांत चोबप आसे व्हंय ?)

Is it right to look at the teeth of a gift-cow ? Cf. Do not look a gift-horse in the mouth.

246. दाय आसताना हात लासचो न्हंय. You should not burn your hand when you have got your spoon. Why worry when you have means ? Similar to Pro. No. 248.

247. दायजी मागता पाड, सोंसो मागता झाड. A cousin wishes ill to his kinsfolk while the rabbit wishes for a tree to lie under. Every animal has an eye for its own gain and comforts.

248. दायी आस्तन हातु लास्सप.
(दाय आसताना हात लासप)

To burn one's hand when one has a spoon (to take out hot curry). Having sufficient means why should one undergo hardship unnecessarily ? Cf. Pro. No. 246.

249. दार काडिना जाल्यार एक अन्यांव. दार काडल्यार हजार अन्यांव. If you do not open the door, you commit only one fault, but if you open it you go in for a thousand faults. It is safe to refuse entrance to undesirable persons though they may blame you for inhospitable conduct; but if you admit them you will have a thousand troubles. Cf. छिद्रेष्वनर्था बहुली भवन्ति.

250. दांत आसताना चणे खांवचे. Eat gram while you have yet teeth. Do things when you have the necessary strength.

251. दांतुय आपले, ऑंठूय आपले. If there is a quarrel between the teeth and the lips we cannot take sides because both belong to us. When our own relations are concerned, we avoid giving judgment notwithstanding we know where the fault lies. दांतही आपले, ऑंठही आपले.

252. दिवडान बेब्याक गिळेल्ल्यावरी. Like a *divad* snake swallowing a frog. The snake swallows a frog without chewing and so this proverb is used when a man takes food without mastication or relish.

253. दिवाळेर तांबडी तोपी. Red cap during the Divali. The meaning is not clear.

254. दिवोडु खावंच्या गांवांतु गेल्लारी मध्य कुट्टुको.
(दिवड खांवच्या गांवांत गेल्यार मदलो कुडको)

If one goes to the village where *divad* snakes are eaten, he should eat the middle part of the snake. Cf. When you go to Rome, do as Rome does.

255. दिव्यांत वात तोंडांत हात. Taking food just when it is getting dark. This is in reference to miserly people who do not keep late at night lest oil should have to be used for lamps.

256. दिसा कैळ्या देकिलारी भिवींची भायल रत्तीची न्हंयी पोवनु वत्ता.
(दिसा कावळो देखल्यार भियेणी बायल रातचां न्हंय पेवन वेता)

The woman who seems to be afraid of a crow in the daytime swims across a swollen river during the night. One who pretends to be a very honest person, robs the royal treasury when he gets the chance.

257. दीपावले पकुट.
(दिव्यावैलें पिसोळें)

A moth hovering round the candle. To court one's death or longing for destruction.

258. दुकर धुयत तितलो चिखलांत लोळटा. The more you wash the pig, the more it rolls in mud. The more you try to clean dirty people, the more dirty they get. स्वभावो दुरतिक्रमः। मूळस्वभाव जाईना.

259. दुकळांत चडित झेनो. Thirteenth month in a famine time, *i.e.*, when we are already in difficulties, we are troubled more if there are further demands on our purse. दुष्काळांत तेरावा महिना.

260. दुडवांचे आशेक गोड विकून गोणी ल्हेंवता. A man sells molasses for the sake of money and licks the bag in which it was kept. This shows the nature of a man who amasses wealth using no portion for his enjoyment.

261. दुड्डु दिवनु चाबूच्या सुण्याक काणु घेवप.
(दुडु दिवन चाबण्या सुण्याक विकतें घेवप)

To buy a biting dog by paying cash. To go in for trouble by inviting it. विकत श्राद्ध.

262. दुद आनी उधाक सरी.
(दुदा-उदका वरी)

Inseparable like milk and water combination.

263. दुद आनी पेयीन्तार सरी.
(दुद आनी साकरे वरी)

Like milk and sugar. To make circumstances more happy or things more enjoyable. Cf Pro. No. 268.

264. दुद पियेवन वीख ओंकचें. Drink milk and vomit poison. This represents the state of mind of an ungrateful man who receives favours but proves treacherous. फणी दुग्धातेंही विजनि गरळातेंचि वमती।

265. दुदाक आइल्ल्याक ह्मशींचें मोल कित्याक ? Why should one ask the price of a buffalo, when he comes to take away her milk ? There are some who are too inquisitive. पाय धू, तर तोडे केवळ्याचे ? बोजा उठाव, तर बाजीराव किदर है ? उचल पत्रावळी, तर जेवणार किती ?

266. दुदाक विर्जण कितलें जाय ? घराक उजो कितलो जाय ? A little butter milk turns milk into curds,and a little fire burns the house. Small accidents end in disaster.

267. दुदा-भूक ताकान. If you cannot get milk to quench your thirst, you have to be content with buttermilk. Be content with what little you get. दुधाची तहान ताकानें भागविणें.

268. दुदांत साकर. Sweetening the milk with sugar, *i.e.*, rendering matters still more relishable. Cf. Pro. No. 263.

269. दुद्देवाली गुर्बा–उधुका–बुळी.
(जुदेवाली गुलाबा-उदका-बुळी)

The rose-water phial of a Jew. This proverb is based on a story. Once a Guru, who might have been perhaps a Jew, asked his disciples to present him with a bottle of rose-water each. They agreed. Every one of them thought that as all the others would bring bottles of excellent rose-water, there would not be anything amiss if he himself gave the Guru a bottle of fresh water ; but unfortunately every disciple thought like that and the Guru got nothing but ordinary water.

270. दुबळ्याक पर्वा ना, पिशाक निद्द ना. A poor man has no worries and a fool cannot sleep. Cf. नंगाकू अल्ला डरता है.

271. दुबळ्याक शेंटां भोव. A poor man gets too many children. दैवो दुर्बल घातकः.

272. दुबळयांच्या भुरग्यांची गोमटी लांब, गिरेस्तांच्या भुरग्यांची जीब लांब. The poor man's children have long necks and rich man's children have long tongues. The poor children poke in everywhere for charity, while the rich children talk too much.

273. देखल्यार चोर नाजाल्यार साव. Thief when caught, otherwise honest. There are persons who pose to be honest, because they have evaded detection. सांपडला तर चोर नाहींतर साव.

274. देखा देखी गांड शेकी. Imitating others without knowing the truth, just as one would warm his buttocks in the sun just because another is doing it. Cf. मोर नाचतो म्हणून लांडोरही नाचते.

275. देवते ज्रोर संभ्रमा पेज. If the Goddess has fever, the servants of the temple get only gruel and no dainties to eat. If those on whom we depend, are in trouble, we have to be content with the little that is vouchsafed to us.

276. देव दिता, देवचार नाट्टा. God gives and the Devil takes away. Often when you luckily get any gains, there arise eventualities which deprive you of your gains. दैव देतें कर्म नेतें.

277. देवाची गेली घांट जाल्यार पुजाऱ्याचें गेलें शेंट. The priest does not care if the temple deity loses the bell. The priest only cares for his own gain. Servants care for themselves more than for their benefactors and masters.

278. देवा-निब्बान भोट्टु खाता.
(देवा-निमतान भंट खाता)

A priest eats because of the deity. Offerings placed before Gods are naturally taken away by the priests present there.

279. दोळाक उधक लावनु फट्टी सांगप.
(दोळ्याक उदक लावन फटी सांगप)

To tell lies after applying water to the eyes. It is commonly supposed that one loses one's eyes if one tells lies; but here is one who wants to protect his eyes by applying water to them when telling lies. This means a confirmed perverse liar.

280. दोळे फुटले म्हुण हिशेब बुडलो? Even if the eyes be blind and you cannot see, the accounts cannot be disputed. Truth

persists even if you do not see it. Cf. कोंबडें झांकलें म्हणून तांबडें फुटावयाचें राहात नाहीं. रविकुक्कुट न्याय.

281. दोळो आसतन दिष्टी न.
(दोळो आसताना दिष्टी ना)

A man cannot see even when he has a good sight (eyes.)

282. दोळ्यां आड मसण पाड. When a thing does not happen in your presence, you do not care and treat it like a desolate burning ground. दृष्टि आड सृष्टि.

283. दोंयालो झाळ. The feast given by Donde (family) who was notorious for making confusion worse confounded, and the invited guests had to go away without any dinner. अन्यवस्थितचित्तानां प्रसादोऽपि भयंकरः This is used when there is a confusion in doing a thing.

284. धर्मांचे गायक दांत ना ओंठ. A gift-cow has neither teeth nor lips. Do not look a gift-horse in the mouth. By way of charity you sometimes get useless things. धर्माचे गाई आणि दांत कांगे नाहीं ?

285. धा जाणांची आवै वाटेर पडून मेली खैं. A mother of ten dies on the road uncared for. Everybody's business is nobody's business. नरहर देवाची पालखी, बारभाईची खेती. Cf. Pro. No. 287.

286. धा जाणांनीं कावळो खावन, खायनाशिल्याक नातीभायर घालो खैं. The ten who ate a crow, have excommunicated the eleventh who has really not eaten the unholy bird. Sinners in a combined majority prove more powerful than the meritorious minority. "Virtue itself, of vice, must pardon beg." (Hamlet).

287. धा जाणांली आवुसु वटेरी.
(धा जाणांली आवै वाटेर)

The mother of ten sons (is forsaken) on the thoroughfare. Everybody thinks that the other son will look after the mother, the result being she has to go begging from house to house. Everybody's business is nobody's business. Cf. Pro. No. 285.

288. धा, जाय तें खा. Eat as much as you like when you are a child ten years old. Small children cannot be prevented from eating as much as they like.

289. धांपिल्ली मूठ लाखाची. A closed fist may contain even a lakh of rupees. You should never advertise your circumstances, especially poverty. झांकली मूठ सव्वालाखाची.

290. धांवतल्याक एकी हादी; सोदित्तल्याक धा.

(धांवतल्याक एकूच वाट; सोदतल्याक धा वाटो)

There is only one way for the man who runs; but there are ten ways for the man who searches for him. This means that it is difficult to catch hold of the man who has run away.

291. धोडयाऱ्याच्या कपाळांत तीन गुंडे. *Dhodyaro* is a kind of fish in whose head three stones are found. However hard an unlucky man may try, he cannot succeed much. घांटावर मेला तरी पळसाला पानें तीनच.

292. नहलें नहा, मेरेथैलें पर्वता. The woman who takes out the weeds, does so without grumbling, but the onlooker sitting on the boundary, grumbles. There are some who grumble for nothing.

293. नण्यारी लग्गले बाघसरी.

(न्हाणार लागिल्ले बाधेवरी)

Like an evil spirit which has haunted a woman while she was having her bath at the completion of her menstrual period. Hindu ladies are untouchable during their menses. On the fourth day, they are given a full bath and then they are allowed to touch things. If an evil spirit or a ghost gets into the body of that woman when she is having her purifying bath, it is said that it is very difficult to get rid of that ghost. This is true. Women are more liable to hysterical manifestations on account of some uterine trouble. This gets aggravated not only on account of want of treatment but on account of the exposure to which the woman is liable by being made to sleep in an open, dirty place, with practically no clothes, and by being compelled to wash her own dirty clothes etc., the result being that her condition is turned from bad to worse.

294. नंका पस्सी व्होड मत्ती.
(नाखापरस व्हड मोतीं)

A nose-ring bigger than the nose. The same idea is expressed in Goa and Karwar side by saying that the pearl is bigger than the nose.

295. न्यायाक नीतीचें बळ, अन्यांवाक धुमक्यांचें बळ. Justice gets strength from morality and injustice from violence. The just are moral and the unjust gain their ends by violent means.

296. नाक नात्तिल्लाकडे कस्तुरी वरप.
(नाख नाथिल्ल्याकडेन कस्तुरी व्हरप)

To take musk to a man who has no nose. To go to a stupid person for enlightenment.

297. नाख कापून अवलक्षण. Cut the nose to spite your face. आपलें नाक कापून दुसऱ्यास अपशकून करणें.

298. नाखटावैल्यान रावण चितारता. Drawing the ten-headed monster Ravana by seeing the nail only. This shows extra cleverness. शितावरून भाताची परीक्षा. स्थालीपुलाक न्याय. सुतानें स्वर्गास जाणें.

299. नाख दांबल्या बगर तोंड उगडना.
नाख धह्यार तोंड उगट्टा.

The mouth is not opened up unless you press the nose. You should attack the weak points in a man and he does submit to you. नाक धरलें म्हणजे तोंड उघडतें.

300. नाखान जेवल्यार पोट भरता ? Your belly cannot be full if you eat with the nose. You have to toil yourself if you want to succeed. Cf. दांत कोरून पोट भरत नाहीं.

301. नाचतल्याचे पांय म्हेळ्टात आनी पळेतल्याचे दोळे वळ्टात. The legs of a person who dances, get soiled, and the eyes of a man who sees, get strained. Those that toil, know the troubles. The wearer knows where the shoe pinches.

302. नाचूंक येना, आंगण वांकडें. If you cannot dance, you blame the ground floor that it is not even. Those that are not well up in their business, blame outside circumstances. Practically similar to the one below.

303. नाच्चूंक कळना जाल्लारी अंगण वांकुडें.
(नाचूंक कळना जाल्यार आंगण वांकडें)

When one does not know how to dance, he finds fault with the court-yard calling it uneven. Cf. A bad workman quarrels with his tools.

304. नारवेंचे चोर. Thieves from Narva. Well-known thieves. Narva is a village in the county of Bicholim-Goa. Cf. पुण्याचा भामटा. Cf. Prov. No. 495.

305. नालकार रडा नालाक, तेलकार रडा तेलाक. The cocoanut dealer cries, for his nuts are too tender, and the oilman cries too, because he does not get full quanity of oil from them. An initial mistake makes everybody suffer. खिळ्यासाठीं नाल गेला. etc.

306. निळू ह्मजो निळू, कोलतेन खेळूं; घर जळ्ळ्यार जळूं पुण निळू ह्मजो खेळूं. Let my Niloo play and play with fire, let him burn the house, but let him play. Over indulgence to a child results in ruin. लाडें झालें वेडें.

307. न्हिदिल्लो न्हिदून गेलो, सोप्यावेल्याचो आंड कापलो. The wrong man was punished for the criminal fault of another. The

adulterer ran away and the man sleeping in the verandah had his balls cut off. Cf. चोरास सोडून संन्याशाला सुळावर चढविणें.

308. नेस्सुंक नज्ज जाल्यरी पिंजुनु पेल्लान घाल्प.
(न्हेसूं नजें जाल्यार पिंजून पेल्यान उडौंप)

To throw away a cloth after tearing it up, because one is not able to wear it *i.e.*, even if a thing is useless to us, certain persons will not give these things to others.

309. पड्टा तो काड्टा. The man who falls, grows also. Unless you experience defeats, you cannot win. Cf. पडेल तो चढेल, बुडेल तो तरेल.

310. पडत पासो जाल्यार खेळत पिसो. When the dice is thrown and comes up favourably, even a fool can play. When circumstances are favourable, even a stupid man gets raised to a position of affluence.

311. पडसी जाल्लेल्या माडारी मोरंक चोल्लोली पडो.
(पडसो जाल्ल्या माडार मरूंक चडलोलो पडलो)

On a palm-tree which was about to fall down, a man climbed up with the idea of courting death. He fell down and died.

312. पडिंग गुंड्यार बीं पिकता? Can you have a produce from a barren stone? Your action if not properly directed, cannot yield any fruit. एरंडाचें गुऱ्हाळ. तृण नाहीं तेथें पडला दावाग्नि, जाय तो विझोनी आपोआप।

313. पतीक पसरो कावार. You ruin your shop if you go on giving samples. You cannot thrive in business unless you are thrifty.

314. परशमन बायल खाली; गजालीन घोव खालो. The husband forgets—when he sits near the hearth for warming himself—all about his wife and household affairs. And the wife forgets all about her husband and the family meals, when engaged in talking with her neighbours.

315. पल्लकेंतु बेस्सुनु भीक मागप.
(पालखेंत बसून भीक मागप)

To go begging when sitting in a palanquin. Cf. A beggar on a horseback.

316. पळ्यात रे दोळ्यांनू, आयकात रे कानांनू, जिबे पापणी मड बंस. Let eyes see and ears hear but let the tongue stop or shut up. Often we must feign ignorance though we may be knowing things. "Give thy ear to all, but to few thy tongue." (Hamlet).

317. पाडे बांयत गांवकार. The headman had concealed himself in a dry well, asking an old woman not to inform anybody of it. But when pressed, the lady who was not a friend of the headman, said 'Do not bother me. The headman might have gone into a dry well.' This is an example of हितशत्रुत्व. Cf. नरो वा कुंजरो वा.

318. पाणबुडो बुडलो तरी सांदन विसरना. The diver does not forget his cakes on which he has set his heart though he may be sinking. There are persons, who will not give up their desires, though they may be in peril.

319. पादाक नांव परमेश्वर. When a rich man does anything nasty, he is praised instead of being taken to task. समर्थांचे घरचें श्वान, त्यासी देती सर्वही मान । नीच रतली रायासी, तीस कोण म्हणेल दासी । जाक विष्टेचे वडपिंपळ, तयासी निंद्य कोण म्हणे ।

320. पादूं पुण नेंदूं. Small faults should be overlooked. पादा पण नांदा.

321. पाद्री पडलो बोवाळाक, इगर्जे नागेली. If the Padre engages himself in activities outside his own sphere, the church will be looted. If you neglect your duties, you will lose your all. अव्यापारेषु व्यापार करणें.

322. पानवेली निमतान झाश्का उदक. पानवेलीच्या धर्मान झास्काक उदक. The otherwise neglected शेगटी tree is watered if the betel leaf creeper is planted at its base. You gain often, if you keep company with those who are cared for. गाड्यावरोबर नळ्याला यात्रा.

323. पावसाक भियेवन न्हंयेंत उडकी मारता. Being afraid of rain, one throws himself into the river. "From frying pan into the fire." सावलीस भितो व भुतास बिलगतो.

324. पांच नागडो नाच. The child is allowed to go naked until he is five years old. लालयेत् पंच वर्षाणि दशवर्षाणि ताडयेत् । प्राप्ते तु षोडशे वर्षे पुत्रं मित्रं समाचरेत् ॥

325. पांय चुकल्यार हतीय पडा. If there be a slip of the foot, even the elephant falls down. Even big men fall, when they lose the balance in business.

326. पायांक लागल्यार पुसून उडोंचें. If you happen to trample on dirty filth, rub it off the foot then and there. Do not carry small things to extremes.

327. पायांचो कांटो काडूंक कुराड किल्याक? Why use an axe to take off the thorn from the foot? Little ailings must have little remedies. नखानें काम होतें तेथें कुऱ्हाड कशाला? नखाहि नको ज्या कार्या, त्या काढावा कशास करवाल?। Cf. Prov. No. 528.

328. पिक्कल्ली खोली पडनाफुडें हरवी खोली हस्सता.
(पिकिली खोली पडनाफुडें हरवी खोली हांसता)

The fresh and green leaf of a tree laughs when the ripe and yellow leaf falls down. The green leaf does not know when it laughs that its fate is the same as that of the yellow leaf and that it will also fall down in course of time. Cf. Prov. No 527.

329. पिंडुक नातिल्ली वडींक.
(पिडुक नायिल्लें लग्न)

A marriage without the auspicious beads. Amongst the Hindus it is absolutely necessary that the bridegroom should tie round the neck of his bride, a neck-lace made of glass and golden beads. This neck-lace the bride must wear on her neck till she dies or becomes a widow. This neck-lace is exempted from attachment under a law-court's decree; so sacred it is considered to be.

330. पिशाच्या हातांत कोलती A fire-brand in the hands of a mad man. If unreliable people are entrusted with responsible work, the result will be disastrous. पिशाचाच्या हातीं कोलीत. Cf. Prov. No. 410.

331. पिशाच्या हातांत दिली वात, रिशें नाचता सगळी रात If you give the lamp in the hands of a demented fool, he will dance the whole night. Those who are undeserving should not be raised to positions of trust. भताचे हातीं कोलीत.

332. पिस्साच्याक समुद्राकडे व्हरप.
(पिशाक समुद्राकडेन व्हरप)

To take a mad man to the sea. To make a greater fool of one who is already so. It is supposed that the sight of the sea—one does not know on what authority—drives one mad

333 पींजिल्ह्यांत पांय, शिजेल्ह्यात दाय. If you happen to entangle your leg in a torn garment, it will be torn the more; so also if you move the spoon too much in the boiled substance, that will spoil the food. It is not proper to render matters worse by fussing over them. Cf. फाटक्यांत पाय.

334. पुनवेंचें चोर आनी उमाशेचें पोर. People think that a child born on the full moondav becomes a thief, and one born on the moon night, dark becomes an orphan.

335. पुर्तुगालें खापुळ. In order to annoy the Portuguese who are fair in complexion, they are called Portuguese Negroes. An insulting expression.

336. पेजेक ा नाशिल्लो शिताक रडा. A man who cannot get gruel, cries for boiled rice. It is no use crying for things beyond your reach.

337. पॅगटभेर उदकांत वचून सुकी काष्टी. He goes in the water thigh-deep and yet his loin-cloth is dry. This is in reference to persons who do all sorts of mischief and yet remain aloof and safe. समुद्रांत राहून कोरडा.

338. पैलीं आइल्ले कान बरे, मागीर आइल्लें शिंग बरें न्हंय. The soft horns which the animal gets first are safer than the horns that sprout later on. "King log is better than the King stork." Cf. पानामागून आली व तिखट झाली.

339. पोट मारून जोत केलें आनी वागान खालें. A farmer bought a pair of bullocks for his plough by starving himself and the pair fell a prey to a tiger. We save at great inconvenience to ourselves, but all of a sudden, a calamity overtakes us and deprives us of all that we have saved. Cf. तेली साची धार धार, खुदा नेतो एकच वार.

340. पोट शिकैता वेव्हार आनी पेठ शिकैता दर. The necessity for food, teaches us how to deal with people and the market teaches the rates of provisions. You learn how to behave, being forced by the circumstances under which you live.

341. पोटाची नळी आनीं कानाची पाळी वाडैत तितली वाडा. If you allow the stomach to grow, it grows like the hole in the lobe of the ear. They both grow and grow. The more you enjoy the greater your wish for enjoyment.

342. पॉवित्यांत मुतूंक बरें. There is a leak in the roof allowing the rain-water to come in; if a man urinates there in that puddle, nobody is the wiser. See preface.

343. फळा तेकीत बीं, धरणी तेकीत उदक. As is the fruit, so is the seed. As is the earth, so is the water. खाण तशी माती, बीज तसा अंकुर. Cf. Prov. Nos. 390 and 484.

344. फाटीर मार, पुण पोटार मारूं नाका. Strike on the back but not on the belly. Do not deprive a man of his means of earning a livelihood. पाठीवर मारा पग पोटावर मारूं नका. Cf. Pro. No. 236.

345. फातर्पेच्यान गोंय लागीं. If you go to the village Fatarpem why don't you go to Goa which is just close by ? काशीला गेलें म्हणजे प्रयाग जवळ.

346. फायी मोर्त्तोलो म्होणु आजी फोंडांतु पडप आस्स वे ?
(फाल्यां मरतलो म्हुण आज फोंडांत पडप आसं व्हय ?)

Is it right to get to-day into a grave, because one has to die to-morrow ? Meet danger when it comes. Do not anticipate it. Cf. Prov. No. 439.

347. फुक्या सवाय तें फुक्या म्हारंग. What is too cheap, is really too dear. "Dear things last well."

348. फुठ उधुक्का फेणु.
(फुक्या उदकाचो फेण)

Lather of plain water. Water by itself cannot produce any lather; so, as fruitless as trying to get lather out of plain water.

349. फुलांच्या झेल्यान माह्लेलें दुखलें, चाबकान माह्लेलें दुखलें ना. You feel, when beaten with a bunch of flowers, but you do not feel when beaten with a whip. Some take small things to heart and pass over greater events. Cf. आवडतीचें मसण गोड. This is in reference to भर्तृहरी's family life.

350. फुलां विकलीं थें वावळ्यो विकच्यो न्हेंयत. Do not sell thread or string where you have sold flowers. When you lose your credit, do not mix with the people who once honoured you ; in fact leave that place altogether. फुलें वेंचलीं तेथें गोवऱ्या वेंचणें.

351. फुलिल्लें फूल परमळनासताना रावना. The flower when it opens out in full bloom, does give out the scent. Good actions are naturally advertised.

352. फेस्त करता गांव, प्रेजिदेन्तीचें नांव. The town celebrates the feast, but the President is applauded for the feast. Undue credit is often given to those in authority though the laborious work is done by others. Cf. आयजीचे जिवावर बायजी उदार.

353. बडये भया खेतें नाचता. The small monkey dances because of the 'beating' cane. Anything done without interest or heart, is useless. Cf. लकडी शिवाय मकडी वळत नाहीं.

354. बडी कातरून कुडके करूं येत; उदक कातरून कुडके करूं येत ? You can cut a stick into pieces, but you cannot cut water into fragments.

355. बरीं फुलां बाजारांत व्हरचीं लागनात. You need not take good flowers to the market. The customers come to you for them. Good things have always a ready market. Good wine needs no bush.

356. ब्रह्मा–मुंजी मंतिल्लो.
(ब्रह्मदेवाली मुंज केल्लो)

One who has celebrated the thread ceremony of Brahmadeva. This proverb means either a very very old and a clever man or one who is considered too clever and an egregious fool.

357. बाणीर बोट. Just as a man placing his finger on the railing of the ship, thinks that the ship is not moving because his finger does not move, there are persons who will stick up to their foolish notions, though circumstances may have changed.

358. बापुय मेल्या वर्सा ओत चड, आवै मेल्या वर्सा भूक चड. The sun is more sultry during the year, the father dies and more hunger during the year, the mother dies. The father is the supporter and the mother is the feeder.

359. बायलांकडेन गूढ सांगूं नाका, रायाकडेन फट मारूं नाका, चौगांचें उतर मोडूं नाका. Don't tell a secret to women, don't tell lies to the King and don't go against the wishes of the majority.

360. बायिल नक्का जळ्ळेल्याक तक्कांतु फातरु एत्ता.
(बायल नाका जाल्लेल्याक ताकांत फातर येता)

One who does not like his wife, finds pebbles in the buttermilk served by her. One finds fault with his wife or with any one else whom he does not like, in season and out of season.

361. बांयतुलें काणु न्हंयींतु.
(बांयतलें काडून न्हंयेंत)

To take a thing from a well and throw it into a river. To recover an object which is lost in the well is difficult; but when it is got at and thrown into the river it is impossible to get it back. This means to overcome some difficulty in the beginning only to find that one has been plunged into greater difficulties impossible to overcome.

362. बांयींतुलो बेब्बो.
(बांयतलो बेबो)

A frog living in a well. One who has no experience of the outside world. कूपमंडुक.

363. बांयींतु बुडलारी न्हंयींतु.
(बांयत बुडल्यार न्हंयेंत)

To dive in a well and get out from a river. This is applied to a very cunning and clever man.

364. बारदेसकारांली वैय. Two Bardescars wanted dry sticks to kindle their fire with. They started a quarrel purposely, and commenced to take out the poles from a neighbouring hedge, as if they were going to beat one another.

365. बारा पोडी बम्मणाक तेरा पोडी बायल.
(बारा पडी घोवाक तेरा पडी बायल)

For a husband who eats twelve measures of rice, there is a wife who eats thirteen measures. An extraordinary personality meets sooner or later another personality who is still more extraordinary. शेरास सवाशेर.

366. बारा वर्साचेन धल्लो करो, ह्मजो कुस्वास बरो. A girl twelve years old, carries a small pot and the mother feels proud of her daughter's prowess.

367. बीं तशें भात. The paddy is like the seed. "As you sow, so you reap." खाण तशी माती. Cf. Pro. No. 194.

368. बुद्धि आस्सिल्ल्याक भंडार जाय वे ?
(बुद्द आशिल्ल्याक भांडार जाय व्हेय ?)

Does a wise man require accumulated treasures? This means wisdom is more valuable than treasure or riches.

369. बेकार मेस्त गांड तासता. A carpenter without work cuts off his own buttocks. This is in reference to persons who having nothing to do, go about playing mischef. रिकामा न्हावी भिंतीला तुंबड्या लावी. Cf. Prov. No. 452.

370. बेताळाक ना बायल आनी भावका देवतेक ना घोव. The Vetal has no wife and the Bhavca Goddess has no husband. These two naked deities are ugly and cannot have proper matches. Hence one is considered to be the match for the other. This is in reference to the brides and bridegrooms who have to be content with the match they procure, because both do not possess any great qualifications. वेताळास नाहीं बायको, भावका देवीस नाहीं नवरा. झसोबास नाहीं बायको, सटवाईस नाहीं नवरा.

371. बोट दिल्यार हात गिळ्टा. If you give the finger, the whole hand is eaten. There are persons who, when they are shown a little consideration, want to take advantage to the fullest extent. भटास दिली ओसरी आणि भट हात पाय पसरी.

372. बोतरार इतलें तर कापडार कितलें? If the woman in rags, brags so much, how much will she brag when she has a good saree to clothe herself. There are persons who are too proud, and in their pride, forget that they have no status in life. Cf. जिनें पाहिला नव्हता दिवा, तिनें पाहिला आवा, तिच्या गर्वा नाहीं ठावा.

373. बोंबशणै करीत ती दिवाळी. It is the privilege of Bomb Shanai to fix the Divali day. "Big men have their whims." Cf. राजा करी ती पूर्व दिशा. भट सांगेल ती अमावास्या.

374. बोंबेचो कोळसो.

375. भटाक गर्वूय ना आनी विद्याय ना. The priest has neither pride nor learning. This is in reference to persons who lack both learning and self-respect. भटास विद्या नाहीं व गर्वही नाहीं.

376. भटो भटो आपल्यो वाटो. The Bhat will mind his own way.. There are persons like the priest who care for their selfish ends. Cf. नवरा मरो नवरी मरो, उपाध्याला दक्षिणेशीं कारण. Cf. Prov. No. 487.

377. भारिल्लो कळसो चकनळना. ' The pot which is brimful does not make any noise. The wise do not prattle. Deep waters make no noise. Cf. This proverb is the opposite of उथळ पाण्यास खळखळाट फार.

378. भरिल्या बामणाक धेंय करकरता. A Brahman who has feasted himself full, finds the curds hard. Those that have their desires fulfilled, do not care for ordinary pleasures and are out for fault-finding.

379. भस्मासुरालो वोरु.
(भस्मासुरालो वेर)

The boon of the Demon Bhasmasura. This special boon instead of helping the Demon burnt him into cinders. Similarly when a person meets disaster by his own actions, we say that he has got the Demon Bhasmasura's boon.

380. भंगरा-कोळस्या कुंकुमे तिळो.
(भांगरा-कळश्या कुकमा-तिळो)

A mark of red powder on a gold vessel. A pot made of gold is very beautiful and when it is adorned with a mark of red powder it becomes still more charming. So when a person has a beautiful form and an excellent character also, he is said to resemble a golden pot with the mark of red powder put on it.

381. भंगरा-वट्टयांतु दुद्दा-पेज.
(भांगरा-वाटयेंत दुदा-पेज)

Milk gruel in a gold saucer. The perfect acme of happiness or prosperity.

382. भंगरा-सूव मोणु दोळांतु गालुं वे?
(भांगरा-सूय ह्मूण दोळयांत घालूं व्हय?)

Shall I thrust a needle into my eyes because it is made of gold? सोन्याची सुरी ह्मणून पोटांत खुपसावी काय?

383. भागुबायच्यो आबोल्यो. Bhagubai put in flowerseeds. The next day she wanted to gather the flowers. People in stupid hurry. Much too impatient. उतावळा नवरा गुडघ्यास बाशिंग पी हळद हो गोरी.

384. भाड्या बैलाक देवा राखण. The bullock on hire has to be cared for, by God, as the hirer neglects it. The orphan must look to God for protection.

अरक्षितं तिष्ठति दैवरक्षितम् ।
सुरक्षितं दैवहतो विनश्यति ॥
आंधळयाच्या गाई देव राखतो.

385. भायर गोरो भित्तरी काळो.
(भायर गोरो भितर काळो)

Outside white but inside black. Cf. A fair face conceals a foul heart.

386. भायीर पोर्वोतु भित्तरी खर्वोतु.
(भायर पर्वत भितर खर्वत)

Outside mountain, inside saw. Outside smooth, inside rough. Do not go by appearances simply.

387. भिकाऱ्याक ओंकारो. A beggar should not show disgust when anything bad is given to him. Beggars should not be choosers. भिकाऱ्यास ओंकारी.

388. भिकाऱ्याकडेन भीक मागल्यार हार्गसेर मार. If you beg of a beggar, he will give you a good thrashing. You cannot get anything out of poverty stricken people. On the other hand they will give you trouble. एकादशीचेकडे शिवरात्र गेली आणि साऱ्या रात्र भर कुडकुडून मेली. Cf. Prov. No. 78.

389. भिकाऱ्याच्या पोराक कोमुर्फेंचें फेस्त As preposterous as the idea of a beggar's son, going to the crowded and big fancy fair of Komurfem.

390. भीं तक्कीत भात्त.
(बीं तसलें भात)

As the seed, so the paddy. Cf. As you sow, so shall you reap. Cf. Prov. Nos. 343 and 484.

391. भुतान घाडी लिपैलो. The ghost has hidden the devil-exorciser. Sometimes those who undertake with confidence, to remove troubles, get themselves into trouble.

392. भुरग्यांचे मळणेक बीं ना भात. When the children thrash the corn there is neither seed nor paddy. This is in reference to ignorant people who cannot be expected to do anything productive of good. मुलांचे मळणीस बीं नाहीं भात.

393. भूक खाता रूख. Hunger eats trees, meaning that a man who is hungry, is not particular for the taste or quality of the food he gets. भुकेस कोंडा, निजेस धोंडा.

394. भैऱ्याफुडें गालें आनी कुड्ड्यामुखार नाचलें, मेळून सारकेंच. Singing before a deaf person and dancing before the blind, both are equally useless. गाढवापुढें वाचली गीता, कालचा गोंधळ बरा होता. Cf. Prov. No. 454.

395. भोंकता तें सुणें चावना, चावता तें सुणें भोंकना. A barking dog never bites and a biting dog seldom barks. Those that look silent are more dangerous than those who threaten much in words. गर्जेल तो वर्षेल काय ?

396. मज्जर नत्तिल्या गांवांतु विन्दुरु रायु.
(माजर नाथिल्ल्या गांवांत हुंदीर राया)

The rat is the King in the land where there are no cats. In the absence of authority the thieves carry on the government. निरस्त पादपे देशे एरंडोपि द्रुमायते.

397. मज्जराक देक्किल्लो किरु.
(माजराक देखिल्लो कीर)

A parrot who has seen a cat; that is one who is frightened or is in a state of fear.

398. माथिलावेलो नाल्लु.
(वण्टीवैलो नाल्ल)

The cocoanut placed on the top of a wall. If a cocoanut is placed on the top of a wall nobody can say whether it will fall inside or outside the wall. Similarly when a person has not joined any particular party he is said to sit on a fence facing both the ways like the cocoanut on the top of a wall.

399. मनशाक उतर, गोरवाक दांवें. Just as the rope ties up the cattle, so does a word tie up a man. Reasoned answers silence many a man.

400. मन्नांतु थायु आस्स जालारि मोच्चुवांतूय थायु आस्स.
(मनांत ठाय आसे जाल्यार मचव्यांतूय ठाय आसे)

If there is room in the mind, there is room in the boat. Cf. Where there is a will, there is a way.

401. मरच्या उठिल्लो घरच्या वळखना. A person who is at the end of his life, does not recognise his kith and kin. The desperate people ruin even their own kith and kin, for their own benefit.

402. मरूंक लागल्यार चेडे उरनात, आनी जेंवक लागल्यार मुडे उरनात. Death takes away sons just as rice-stock is exhausted when it is being eaten up every day. Cf. आदा नसताना खर्च.

403. मंकटा हत्तांतु माणिक.
(माकडा हातांत माणिक)

As useless as a ruby in the hands of a monkey. A monkey does not know the value of a jewel. Cf. Prov. No. 524.

404. ह्याज्या घरा बारां जोतां, पुण हांव भीक मागून खातां. Our house has twelve pairs of oxen for the ploughs, but I am living on charity. There are some who however rich, allow their dependents to live in abject poverty.

405. ह्मशी फाट्टीरी पावसु.
(म्हशी फाटीर पावस)

Rain on the back of a she-buffalo. It is said that when the rain falls, the buffalo feels a great pleasure; so when a person is very much pleased, this expression is used. See Prov. No. 455.

406. म्हशी-शिंग म्हशीक जड? The horns of the buffalo are not heavy to the buffalo, just as the fruit of the creeper is not burdensome to the creeper. However poor we may be, our children are not burdensome to us. Cf. Prov. No. 477. म्हैशीची शिंगें म्हैशीस जड होत नाहींत.

407. म्हैस घेंवक सोपें आनी दांवें घेंवक जड. Easy to buy a buffalo, but difficult to buy a rope to tie her with. Do not undertake anything unless you understand the future responsibilities. Cf. लग्न करावें पाहून (पुढच्या अडचणी पाहून).

408. म्हैस वियेता आपले खाजीक. The buffalo brings forth a calf not for giving milk to others. म्हैस फळते ती धन्याला दूध देण्यासाठीं फळत नाहीं.

409. म्हसी-वांसराक झडिच्यांतु लेखिलें वे ?
(रेडकाक कैरांत लेखलें व्हय ?)

Do you consider that the buffalo-calf is of no account because it is among the rubbish that is swept away? Do you consider a jewel as of no value simply because it has fallen in the rubbish?

410. माकडा-हाता उज्या-कोलती. A firebrand in a monkey's hand. Evil powers in the hands of persons devoid of reasoning. माकडाच्या हातीं कोलीत. Cf. Prov. No. 330.

411. माजर गू लिपैता. The cat hides its dung. There are persons who draw a curtain over their evil deeds.

412. माजरा बोडावेली पोणत्ती.
(माजरा-बोडावैली पण्टी)
(माजरा-बोडावैलो दिवो)

Earthen light placed on the head of a cat is sure to fall down. This is used when matters are arranged in such a way that they are sure to tumble down. Unsteady.

413. मांजोराला फुलां. If you even touch the flowers in the Major's garden who is the local commandant, the consequences are awful.

414. माडाक आनी माडयेक एकुची खडु.
(माडाक आनी माडयेक एकूच खाडूं)

To use the same *Khadu* or circular loop of a cord for climbing both the cocoanut as well as arecanut trees. *Khadu* is a circular loop of a rope used in climbing palm-trees, etc., which is placed on the feet and a purchase obtained in climbing up. To use the same sized loop for climbing the stout cocoanut tree as is used to climb up the very small trunk of a arecanut tree is practically impossible. So, this proverb means that it is stupid to apply the same standard in measuring two different objects which have broad inherent differences in them.

415. मानेवैले कॅंस फाटीर नाजाल्यार पोटार. The hair on the neck will naturally fall on the back or on the stomach. One's own children and relatives have to be helped and supported somehow or other; they cannot be left to their fate.

416. माये बगर रॅड ना, उज्या बगर कॅड ना. There is no real weeping unless there is love. No boiling of the water without fire. Tears naturally flow when you have love for the object for which you weep. माये शिवाय रड नाहीं, जाळाशिवाय कड नाहीं. मोलें घातलें रडाया, नाहीं असूं आणि माया.

417. मारांक भूत पळटा. The devil is afraid of the cane. This is from the practice of the exorciser who tries to drive the devil away by giving a sound thrashing to the person possessed.

418. म्हातारी जाल्यार जांव बावडी, घराक आधार आस. Never mind if she is too old. She at least watches the house. Every trivial article even is useful. The grass shows how the wind blows.

419. म्हातारी बोडकी वड्यांक उपकारता. The old widow is useful for frying small cakes. तृणेन कार्यं भवतीश्वराणाम्.

420. म्हाताऱ्या बैला गुणवन्ता. The old bullock is always good-natured. Old age can give good advice when it can no longer set bad example by deeds. With the passing away of youthful pranks and vices, a man becomes virtuous in his after life. वृद्धा नारी पतिव्रता.

421. म्हाळ्काराल्या घराकडेन गोरूं सांडलां. To go to the house of the man who is giving a feast in honour of his ancestors, on the excuse that his cattle has strayed that side; but the real object is to cadge for an invitation. Cf. अगे अगे म्हशी मला कां नेशी ! Cf. Prov. No. 466.

422. मिसयेक घंट्टो मंधिल्लो.
(मिशयेक घांट बांदिल्लों)

One who has tied bells to his moustaches. This is in reference to a man of extraordinary abilities.

423. मीठ खेल्लेलो उधाक पित्तोलो.
(मीठ खाल्लोल्लो उदक पियेतलो)

One who has eaten salt will have to drink water. He who commits a crime will be punished even after a long time.

424. मुहुर्त्ता वेळेरी सस्समयी पिर्डुकयी एक करप.
(म्हुर्ता वेळार सांसवां पिर्डुको एक करप)

To mix mustard seeds and beads at the auspicious moment. As mustard seeds and pirdukas (glass-beads) are of the same size and colour it is very difficult to separate them easily. At the time of a marriage which must take place at a particular auspicious moment, a necklace of these glass-beads, etc., must be tied round the neck of the bride; if it be not done so at the very moment, some harm or misfortune is likely to befall either the bride or the bridegroom; hence the necessity of getting ready a necklace of those beads. Cf. To make confusion worst confounded.

425. म्हुर्त ल्हान पुण कीर्त व्हॅड. The idol is small but the reputation is great. Sometimes seemingly small men achieve great reputation. मूर्ति लहान पण कीर्ति मोठी.

426. मुंडो खेल्लेल तोंडान कुंडो खावप.
(मुंडो खाल्ल्या तोंडान कुंडो खावप)

Eating bran by the same mouth which had eaten the sweet *mundo* (a kind of sweetmeat prepared from wheat-flour, sugar etc). This means to fall low from great affluence.

427. मूळय वल्लीय नात्तिल्लो.
(मूळ आनां वालूय नाथिल्लो)

Having neither root nor stem. One without beginning or end or one whose descent cannot be known. Cf. Prov. No. 132.

428. मेजावैलें केळें काडून फिर्याद जेाड्टा. Remove the plantain from the table of another man and file a complaint against that man. This shows how some create cases for litigation. The Konkani people are supposed to be very fond of litigation and create unnecessary intricacies.

429. मेल्ल अम्मा-दुद पिल्लोलेा.
(मेले अंबे-दुद पियेल्लो)

One who has drunk the milk of a dead mother—means a fool. I am not one who has drunk the milk of a dead mother means I am not a fool.

430. मेल्ल म्हशीक बारा शेर दुद. When the buffalo dies, you say it yielded twelve seers of milk. Lavished praise to the dead मेल्या म्हैशीस दहा शेर दुध.

431. मेल्लेल म्हसीक दुद चड.
(मेले म्हशीक दुद चड)

A dead she-buffalo gave plenty of milk. The owner demands a very high price for a buffalo accidentally killed stating that the buffalo gave plenty of milk. The buffalo being dead there is no possibility of proving how much milk was got from the animal.

432. मेळ्यान मोग वाडिता.

433. मैरेंची पिसाय. As great a fool as the people of Moira, a village in Bardez-Goa, who try to collect the sun rays in a barrel so that they may have sunshine in the rainy weather.

434. मोगाची मावशी चांदन्याक उवो मारता. The aunt is so very loving that she goes to the length of picking out the lice from the head of her niece, even during moon-light.

435. मोडाक खोंचप-
(मड्याक बडैाप)

To beat a dead body. To do a thing which is productive of no good whatsoever.

436. मोडा-तोण्णांतुली लाळ लेंवप.
(मड्या-तोंडांतली लाळ ल्हेंवप.)

To lick the saliva that oozes out of the mouth of a dead body. To be stingy or miserly even to the last degree. Cf. Prov. No. 153.

437. मोव आसं थैं खणटा. Digging where the ground is soft. To take undue advantage. Harassing the weak. मऊ सांपडलें म्हणून कोपरानें खणूं नये.

438. मोवु आस्सीक्कडे खोणप.
(मोव आशिल्लेकडेन खणप)

To dig where the ground is soft. To press where it would yield.

439. येत्तल्ल जन्म सुणें नात्तोलो म्होणु ये जन्म गू खवप आस्स वे ?
(येतल्या जल्मा सुणें जातलो म्हुण ह्या जल्मा गू खावप आसं व्हय ?)

Would it be right to eat dung in this life because one is destined to be born a dog in the next life? One does not understand why the dog is introduced into this proverb. The dog never goes in for dung. Cf. Prov. No. 346.

440. येना मागूंक भीक जाल्यार घुडगुडी ओडूंक शीक. If you know not how to beg, learn to smoke hubble-bubble. (This habit invariably leads a man to beg for tobacco, etc.). Vices and bad habits make us lose our self-respect. भीक मागतां येईना तर बैदिकी (or वैद्यकी) शीक.

441. येन्यान गेलें ना जाल्यार हुणयेन गेलें. The boat sank. It does not matter the least bit which end went in first. Unprofitable and vexatious wrangling. वितंडवाद

442. यो गे लुडबे, वच गे लुडबे. Coming and going aimlessly. To spend time without any definite object.

443. रडत रावत घोड्यार. A weeping soldier riding a horse. Cowards cannot make fighters. रडत राऊत घोड्यावर.

444. रब्बुनु मुत्तुच रय्याक, धांवनु मुत्तुचो मंत्री.
(उब्यांनीं मुतण्या रायाक धांवन मुतणो मंत्री)

The king who urinates by standing, has a minister who urinates when running. This is in reference to a wicked king who has a more wicked minister.

445. रवळनाथाचें कूळ. Ravalnath is supposed to be a very poor deity; hence his devotees are considered to be wretched.

446. राजालें धुपाटणें मडवळालें गांड पुसणें. The king's towel is the washerman's cloth for cleaning buttocks. The servants sometimes misuse the master's possessions, because these are temporarily in their charge. Cf. Dhobi's itch which is carried from the Dhobi using his master's clothes, back to the master.

447. राय्याल्या खण्डाक दोन्नीय तंतु दार.
(रायाले तरवारीक दोंयवशीन धार)

A king's sword is sharp on both the sides. The king can do anything, right or wrong. Even if he does something wrong, people say that he is right.

448. रावणाक भिकेचे दुवाळे. Ravana the richest king of Lanka wished to act as a beggar, when he wanted to kidnap the Goddess Seeta. The rich often take pleasure in the meanest of acts and bring disaster on themselves. राजाला भिकेचे डोहाळे.

449. रावणाक सत्ते धाल्लोंलो.
(रावणाक सांतली धल्लोलो).

One who had held an umbrella for Ravana. A man of extraordinary capacity.

450. रांड भीण ह्मणात, पोटभर वाढात. Call me all sorts of names but give me a full meal. Cf. कुंकू लावा व सवाष्ण ह्मणा.

451. रांदपिणीलो पोर उपाशीं मरना. The cook's son will not starve for want of food; because she has the food in her possession. Those that possess wealth, make provision for their own kith and kin before they satisfy outside creditors. Cf. तळें राखी तो पाणी चाखी. Cf. Prov. No. 219.

452. रिकामी मेस्त बायलेचे बुले ताशी. A carpenter without work chops off the buttocks of his wife. Persons who do not engage themselves in good work, do things which are productive of evil. Cf. Prov. No. 369. रिकामा न्हावी कुडाला तुंबड्या लावी.

453. रिबेर बावरीसो वावुरता. He works as hard as a galley-slave. (Ribeira=The place where the galley-slaves used to work in the old city of Goa).

454. रेड्या–गांडी कडेन किनरी. Playing the flute near the buttock of the buffalo. It is useless to sing to persons who cannot appreciate it or give advice to persons who have no sense. Cf. गाढवाला गुळाची चव काय ? Cf. Prov. No. 394.

455. रेड्यार पावस पड्टा. It is raining over the buffalo. This is waste of rain. The proverb shows how sometimes good things are wasted over bad people. रेड्याचे पाठीवर पाऊस. See Prov. No. 405.

456. रेवें हंचो विणप.

(रेवेंचो राजू वळप)

To weave ropes out of sand. Cf. To extract oil out of sand.

457. लग्न जालो ना म्हूण आटवा पोंदसून गेलो ना ? Supposing a man has not got himself married, has he not been under a decorated shamiana put up for somebody's wedding ? Though a man may not have actual experience, he can have knowledge.

458. लज्जेक गेल्लारी पेज्जेक विघ्न.
(लजेक गेल्यार पेजेक विघ्न)

Bashfulness endangers gruel. Bashfulness stands in the way of earning bread. This proverb is used when persons show some sort of shame or bashfulness in doing certain duties which, they think are below their dignity. Cf. लज्जेक आर्नी पेजेक पडना.

459. लज्जेक आनी पेजेक पडना. If you are too bashful you will not get gruel to drink. When you want to gain your object, you must push on with zeal and even with immodesty. Too much bashfulness is the sister of beggary. A man who is too bashful does not succeed in life. Cf. लज शिकेच्ची भैण. थीड शिकेची बहीण.

460. लस्सुल्लारी तेल.
(लाशिल्लयार तेल)

To pour oil on the burning material. To add fuel to the fire. Cf. आगींत तेल.

461. लाशिल्ल्या उंगट्यार मुतना. He will not even make water on a toe burnt. Extremely selfish.

462. लास्सल मासळेक कुस्सली चिंच.
(लशिले मासळेक कुशिल्ली चिंच)

Rotten tamarind for the burnt fish. We use this proverb when a man who is very bad, gets an equally bad mate Cf. Pro. No. 117.

463. लोणयांतुलो अग्गोळु.
(लोणयांतलो आगोळ)

A tress of hair taken from butter. It is said that no butter will adhere to a tress of hair even if it be kept there for some time.

464. लोणी आस्स जाल्लारी तूप कोरूंक तोटोवु आस्स वे ?
(लोणी आसे जाल्यार तूप करूंक कळाव आसे न्हंय ?)

Will there be any delay to make ghee if there is butter ? When the means are available, the result is easy.

465. वट्टे आस्सुनु कट्टे काउप.

(वाटी आसून कट्टी काउप)

To use cocoanut shells when one has got plates. To live miserly when one has got riches.

466. वर्डीके मंटपांतु पाड्या सोधुनु आयला.

(लग्न-माटवांत पाडो सोदूंक आयला)

He has come to the wedding pandal in search of a bullock. The bullock will not come into the marriage pandal where there are many people. The man who comes into that pandal on the excuse that he has come to search for his bullock, will be the one who was not invited for the marriage and is trying to cadge an invitation. Cf. Prov. No. 421.

467. व्हडान खाल्यार ओखताक, दुबळ्यान खाल्यार पोटाक. If big people eat anything bad, it is said to be eaten as medicine But if the same is eaten by poor people, it is supposed to be eaten to appease hunger. The world defends rich men's wrong doings and exposes those of the poor. मोठ्यानें खाल्लें तर औषधासाठीं; लहानानें खाल्लें तर पोटासाठीं.

468. वाग पडलो धाळी केल्दें दाखैता नाळी. If the tiger is caught, the monkey also insults him. When powerful men are in difficulties, the weakest try to flout their authority पिंजरीं जरी व्याघ्र सांपडे, बायका मुलें मारिती खडे ।

469. वागाची मावशी. The aunt of a tiger is the cat. Indirect way of calling a woman a cat.

470. वागा-पोटा कोलो जल्मा आयला. A fox given birth to by the tiger. This is in reference to sons who do not attain the worth and glory of their parents. हिऱ्याच्या पोटीं गारगोटी. सिंहाचे पोटीं कोल्हा.

जातोऽसि कृतविद्योऽसि दर्शनीयोऽसि पुत्रक ।
यस्मिन्कुले त्वमुत्पन्नो गजस्तत्र न हन्यते ॥
सूर्याचे पोटीं शनैश्वर.

471. वाघा–तोण्णांतली गायी.

(वागा–तोणांतली गाय)

A cow from the mouth of a tiger. To do something as hazardous as snatching the cow from the mouth of a tiger. Cf. Prov. No. 540.

472. वाजता थैं गाजता. Where there is the noise of music there must be some ceremony there. Smoke where there is the fire.

473 वांज विर्येवक आनी दुर्कळ येंवक एक जालें. Just as the barren woman brings forth a child, there is famine declared. Sometimes when we get things with difficulty, there are good many troubles attending on it. Cf. वोडकीचे लग्नास सतरा विघ्नें.

474. वाटेन वच्या वागा, मका येवनु खा गा.

(वाटेन वचण्या वागा, म्हाका येवन खा गा)

(वाटे वैल्या वागा म्हाका येवन खागा)

Oh you tiger passing by the way, come and eat me. This means inviting calamity before it actually comes to one Cf. आव कुत्ता मेरेकू काट.

475. वान वोचुनु मधळ्यालगगी सांगता.

(वायन वचून म्हादळ्याक सांगता)

The stone-mortar goes and tells its troubles to the drum (which is like मृदंग and which is beaten from both sides). The mortar receives blows from the pestle in one direction only, while the drum is beaten on both the sides. Persons who have suffered much, seek consolation from those who have suffered much more.

476. वारें चोवुनु मोट्ट मंदप.

(वारें चोवन मोट बांदप)

To tie one's baggage after seeing the nature of the wind and so make ready to start. Before undertaking any work look out for surrounding circumstances.

477. वाली-फळ वालीक जड ! The fruit hanging on a creeper is not found burdensome by the creeper. However poor one may be his children are not considered in any way as a burden by him. Cf. Prov. No. 406.

478. विंदुरान आलें खेळावरी.
(हुंद्रान आलें खाल्ल्यावरी)

Like a rat who has eaten ginger. When a rat swallows ginger he gets out of sorts; similarly when a person is placed in an awkward position we say that his condition is as bad as that of a rat who has eaten ginger.

479. विंदुरु आनी मज्जारु.
(हुंदीर आनी माजर)

Cat and rat. Natural enmity like that of the cat and the rat.

480. विंदुळ्यावेलें गीत कीर्तनांतु येवुना.
(झोंपाळ्यावैलें गीत कीर्तनांत येना)

Songs sung on the swinging bed, do not occur in the celebration of worship of a god. Love-songs cannot be used at the time of singing devotional songs in praise of a deity. Everything has its appropriate place and time. Cf. Prov. No. 485.

481. वीस करता खिसमीस. A man aged twenty gets unsettled on account of love matters.

482. वेगळाल मंटपांतु धाराळत्व.
(परक्याल्या माटवांत उदारपण)

To be extravagant in another's pandal. To enjoy excessively at other's expense. आईजीच्या जीवावर बाईजी उदार.

483. वेगळ्याला दंतापस्सी अवंगेलो ओणुव चंगयों.
(दुसऱ्याल्या दांतापरस आमगेली दाड बरी)

One's own jaws are better than the teeth of others. The teeth of some one else will not be of any use to us when w are taking our meals. In case we have no teeth, our own jaws will help us in chewing our food. Self-help is the best help

484. वेल तशें फळ. Fruit according to creeper. Cf. As is the fruit so is the seed. Cf. Prov. Nos. 343 and 390.

485. वेळार वेळ शिगम्यार खेळ. We must do things in their proper times. Same way as we are allowed to throw coloured water during the Shimga holidays, and not at any other time. Cf. Prov. No. 480.

486. वैपे वच्चुनु काप्पणी करप.
(वायपी वचून कापणी करप)

To get oneself shaved by going to Vaipi. Vaipim is a village to the north of Cochin harbour and those who require to go over there have to spend two annas as ferry crossing charge; Now those living at Cochin have to pay two annas to the barber but the barber's charge at Vaipim is only one anna; so, in order to save one anna, a man crosses over to the other side and gets shaved there and spends three annas in all. Cf. Pennywise and pound foolish.

487. वोरेतु बोंडिक्की जावो, वोक्कल बोंडिक्की जावो; बडीमट्टा दुडु हत्तारी उडुयी.
(न्हवरो बोडको जाव, हौकल बाडकी जांव; भटा–हातार दुडू उडै)

Let the bridegroom be a widower or the bride be a widow; give the priest his money, *i.e.*, his fees into his palm. This shows the utter selfishness of the priests. Cf. Prov. No. 376.

488. शणैचो जांवैं चुनो खाता, चुनो खाता; तोंड फोपेलें. The Shanai's son-in-law was flattered that he could eat chunam, and in order to satisfy the flatterers he went on eating chunam and the mouth had inflammation. This is in reference to persons who fall victims to flattery and make fools of themselves. हरभऱ्याच्या झाडावर चढविणें.

489. शाण्याक उतरां–मार, पिशाक चाबका–मार. The wise man is punished by words and a fool by a whip. Different persons feel differently according to temperament. शाहाण्यास मार शब्दाचा आणि मूर्खास मार चाबकाचा.

490. शाण्याक तींकडेन, पिशाक एकेव्डेन. The ordinary man gets his foot dirtied; he simply wipes it. But the overwise man removes the dirt with his finger and smells it; so, his foot, finger and the nose get dirty. Cf. अति शहाणा त्याचा बैल रिकामा.

491. शिगमो सल्लो कवतां उल्लीं. The Shimga festivities are over, but the songs remain. This is in reference to a condition of poverty or distress, after riches or happy circumstances pass away. शिमगा गेला पण कवित्व राहिलें. काळ जाय पण केहवत रहे.

492. शिगम्यांत पावस चौथींत गीम. Rain during the Shimga holidays, and summer at the Ganpati festival. This is in reference to unseasonable and wrong happenings.

493. शितां आसल्यार भुतां जायतीं. The devils throng, if you throw to them ample food to eat. Flatterers and friends flock about an opulent man. शितें जोंवरी भुतें भोंवतीं, कोण कुणाचा सखा जिवा. असतील शितें तर मिळतील भुतें.

494. शिर्ल्ये मणके रगत पिवप. Drinking blood like a lizard. It is said that lizards drink blood from a man's body by sitting at a distance. This is in reference to a man who is a parasite.

495. शिवकंचीचें चोर. Thieves from Conjeevarum known as शिवकंची. दिल्लीचा सोदा. पुण्याचा भामटा. Cf. Prov. No. 304.

496. शीत शिजुनु पेज जल्ली.
(शीत शिजून पेज जाली)

The boiled rice became gruel by over-boiling. Rice is put in a vessel with water to boil; after some time the water is poured away ; if it be not done so, the whole thing will be turned into gruel. This means that there is a time-limit for everything.

497. शेजारची हॉकल कुड्डी. The bride in the neighbourhood is blind. A prophet is no prophet in his own land. शेजारची नवरी कुडी. पिकतें तेथें विकत नाहीं.

498. शेट पडल्यार भेट धांवता, भेट पडल्यार कोण धांवता ? If the seth or big man falls down, the Bhat (priest) runs up to him, but if the Bhat should fall, who runs up to save him ? The rich men are always attended to and the poor are neglected.

499. शेट रिवणां सांतली कुसमणां. The goldsmith is at one village while his umbrella is at another village.

500. शेट शृंगारता म्हणसर बाजार उलगलो. By the time the goldsmith dresses himself (to go to the market) the market is over. This is in reference to persons who are behind the time in doing their things and thus lose the bargain. Cf. वराती मागून घोडें.

501. शेटीन कान तोंपिल्लो बरों. If the goldsmith pricks the ear, it is alright. While we complain about bad treatment by some, we don't complain of it when those who are fit by position, give that treatment. सोनारानें कान टोंचणें.

502. शेराक सवायशेर. One and a Quarter seer beat one seer. Turbulent persons cow down before those who are more so. शेरास सवाशेर.

503. शेळ शीत निवांचो.
(शेळें शीत न्हिवैणो)

One who makes cool the already cold rice. This means one who goes in doing unnecessary things.

504. शेंगाडी शिपायक. Cowardly soldier. शेंदाड शिपाई.

505. शें थें सनायशें, कळंतरा खैंचें सें ? Why not borrow 125 in place of 100 ? What of the interest ? Reckless borrowers do not care for interest and borrow beyond necessity.

506. सगळीं बोटां सारकीं नासतात. All the fingers are not equal. Though children of the same parents, there is difference in their character, nature, etc. पांची बोटें सारखीं नसतात. मूर्ति तितक्या प्रकृति.

507. सगळें मुसळ केरांत. The whole of the pounding-rod which is heavy, was swept away with other sweepings. This is in reference to persons who are very careless. सगळेंच मुसळ केरांत.

508. सडुयाची धांव कंयेमेरेन. The chameleon—a short lizard—can run only up to the hedge. Small men cannot achieve much. सरड्याची धांव कुंपणापर्यंत.

509. सत्तेफुडें शाणपण चलना. Wisdom or reason has to bend low before authority. Might is right. सत्तेपुढें शहाणपण नाहीं.

510. सत्याक केतनाय बार वर्ष.
(सत्याक केन्नाय बारा वर्सो)

Truth is always twelve years old. Truth is always truth. Truth alone conquers. सत्यमेव जयते.

511. संदीक सापूस. A sort of first aid. To try to do something to afford relief for the time being.

512. सब्बारी किळक्कारी गेल्लारी पोर्वोतु आस्स.
(सावार उदेतेक गेल्यार पर्वत आसं)

If one goes too much to the east there is a mountain. There is a similar proverb in Malayalam. It is said that this proverb came into existence when the Gaud Sarasvats settled on the sea-coast of Cochin and Travancore which country is bounded on the east by a range of the Malaya mountains ; one does not however understand the peculiar significance attached to it.

513 सब्बारी जालारी विकट.

(साबार जाल्यार विकट)

Too much is bad. Too much of anything results into something bad. अति सर्वत्र वर्जयेत्.

514. समुद्र पोवनु पावलवरी उधुकांतु मेलो.

(समुद्र पोवन पावलभर उदकांत मेलो)

Having swam across the ocean, he got drowned in the water which was only ankle-deep. This means that having survived gigantic difficulties he lost his life by trying to overcome a small obstacle.

515. समुद्रा-फळ. A fruit of the ocean. An Utopean scheme or idea.

516. सवाय तांगाची गवाय. False witnesses bought at the rate of nearly seven pice each. (A *savai tang* is equal to 20 pies.)

517. सवायेचें खाण पोटफुगें. Cheap things are dear in the end. Things cheap are always spoiled and produce colicky pains when eaten.

518. साट बुद्द नाट. A man is supposed to lose his intelligence or sense at the age of 60. साठी बुद्धि नाठी.

519. सार्टी वर्सांनीं सुट फुल्ल्या. A good auspicious occasion after a good many years. कपिलाषष्टीचा योग.

520. सांकव्वारी चोडोवनु फळें ताणप.

(सांकवार चडौन फळें ताणप)

To pull the plank after making one get on the bridge made up of those planks. To encourage a man in starting on an adventure and then to do all sorts of harm to him.

521. सांडिल्ल्याचें मन धांकडेस. If a man has lost anything, he thinks it may have been lost at ten places. One tries a number of ways to gain back what one has lost.

522. सितारेन ह्मॉव काडल्यार तोंडांत पडा ? If we try to take out honey with a long pole, it does not get into the mouth. There is no royal road to success. श्रमाविण फळ नाहीं. Cf. Prov. No. 232.

523. सुके गांडीक ओलो बिबो. To give medicine to one who is healthy. This is used in reference when we misuse a thing.

524. सुगाक सोघोळो नाळ्.
(सुण्याक सगळो नाल्ल)

A whole cocoanut given to a dog. If a dog is given a husked cocoanut, it will not be able to get at the kernel and so eat it; therefore it is of no use to him. Similarly if anything is given to a person, which is of no use to him, we use this proverb. Cf. Pro. No. 403.

525. सुणें संतांतु गेल्लावरी.
(सुणें सांतेंत गेल्यावरी)

Like a dog gone to a market. A dog will not be able to purchase things for us even if it be sent to the market. In the same way when a person returns from a mission without doing anything, we call him as good as a dog sent to a market.

526. सुण्याची शेपडी नळयेंत घाली तरी वांकडी. The tail of a dog continues to be crooked even if it be placed in a hollow straight tube. Wicked people do not change their nature कुत्र्याचें शेंपूट नळींत घातलें तरी वांकडेंच.

527. सुपांतले हांसतात, ओळ्ळ्तले रडात. Those (rice-grains) in the winnowing flat basket laugh, while those rice-grains about to be put in the boiling water for being turned into cooked rice, cry. Those out of danger for the time being, cannot realise the misery of those who are in danger. Cf. Prov. No. 328.

528. सुयेन काडींचें खोरान.
(सुयेन काडचेलें खोऱ्यान)

To use a hoe for the work which can be done with a needle. Cf. Prov. No. 327.

529. सुवे मोन्नारी रब्ववप.
(सुये–तोंकार रावप)

To make one stand on the point of a needle. To maintain a high discipline and order.

530. सुंबु नत्तिल्लें मंधप.
(सुंब नाशिल्लें बांदप)

To tie without using cords. This is in reference to a man who without being tied with cords, feels the pain of bondage or slavery.

531. सून गोटो खायना, मडकेंत कांय ना. The mother-in-law praises her daughter-in-law for her delicate appetite, but her cooking pots are practically empty. This shows that the so-called delicate daughter-in-law must have polished off all the cooked food in the house. Cf. माझें जेवण चुलींत.

532. सूंब जळ्ळें तरी वेळ वचना. Even if the coir-rope is burnt, the shape is not destroyed. There are persons who, however much they may be punished, will not give up their bad habits. सुंभ जळेल, पण पीळ जळणार नाहीं

533. सोबलें बांयत पडलें, पुण कोबलें नितळ जालें. A Christian woman who never washed herself, fell down into a well and came out with her hair clean.

534. हत्ता–कट्टोक कण्णटी जाय वे ?
(हाता–फोडाक हारसो जाय व्हय ?)

Do you want a mirror to see the boil on your hand ? Do you require any evidence when you know that a certain thing has actually taken place ?

535. हती पादता, हती पादता फुस्स. When a big animal like an elephant passes wind, people naturally expect that there would

be a big noise. But there was none. Great expectations end in smoke. The mountain in labour. भ्रमाचा भोंपळा फुटणें.

536. हर झळ्यार बर. Ask one to do something; he does something else.

537. हेंर हेंर झण्टले खूब; खणींत उडकी मारतलो कोण ना. There are a good many who give you lip-sympathy, but there is nobody who will jump into a pit to help you.

538. हस्ति सुकलारी गोट्यांतु मंधप आस्स वे ?
(हतीं सुकल्यारूय गोठ्यांत बांदप आसं व्हंय ?)

Can an elephant who is reduced and become thin, be put into and kept tied in a cow-shed ? Great persons even when they have lost their influence, cannot be regarded as men of no importance.

539 हस्तीक घांट मंधुका वे ?
(हतयाक घांट बांदूंक जाय व्हंय ?)

Is there any need of tying a bell on an elephant ? The elephant is such a big animal that there is no need of tying a bell round its neck to warn people of its coming. This means that there is no need of advertising the merits of a great personality.

540. हस्ती-तोंडांतुलो कोब्बु.
(हतया-तोंडांतलो कबू-उंस)

The sugar-cane from the mouth of an elephant. As impossible as to get a sugar-cane from the mouth of an elephant. Cf. Prov. No. 471.

541. हस्ती नास्तिल्ले आरत.
(हती नाथिल्ली आरंथ)

An *arat* (waving of lamps) without an elephant. After the God's worship is over, it is customary with the Hindus to put small lamps in a dish and wave it before the idols singing at the same time, the special attributes of that God. On the Travancore side, however, it seems to be the custom that these lamps should be waved by an elephant, especially in big and rich temples.

542. हस्ती–संगांतु मुंबुर.
(हतयां–हिंडांत मुसक)

A mosquito in a herd of elephants. दर्यांनें खसखस.

543. हागन्याफुडें वागरें खैंचें ? If a man has a strong desire to relieve himself, he does not care even if there be a tiger near by. Cf. कामातुराणां न भयं न लज्जा.

544. हाण्डीर आसं चेडो, सोदता सगळो वाडो. The child is on her waist and the mother searches for the child in the village. There are persons so absent-minded that they do not know their own mind and behave foolishly. खाकेंत कळसा गांवांत वळसा.

545. हात–पांय रावले, किर्ते करूं बायले ? Now that I am grown infirm and cannot work, what am I to do my wife ?

546. हार उट्टा म्हुण गांयडोळ उट्टा. Because a big serpent jumps, the small insignificant worm jumps up too. It is no use imitating those who are far above you.

547. हालता त्या फातरार उबें रांवचें न्हंय. Do not stand on a shaky rock. Take your stand on solid foundation, *i. e.*, try to get support from really substantial quarters.

548. हांतरूण पळौन पांय पातळांवचे. Before spreading your legs, see how long the bed is. Cut your coat according to your cloth. अंथरूण पाहून पाय पसरणें. ऐपतीच्या मानानें खर्च ठेवावा.

549. हांव हांसतां देसाक, देस हांसता म्हज्या भेसाक. I laugh at the country, and the country laughs at my dress. While we laugh at others, the others ridicule our defects.

550. हांव हांसतां लोकांक, शेंबुड म्हज्या नाखाक. I laugh at others when there is a mucous secretion running from my nose.

Cf. you see a mole in the eyes of others, but not a beam in your own. Some find fault only with others and forget their own. आपण हांसे लोकाला, शेंबूड आपल्या नाकाला. Cf. Prov. No. 21.

551. हुंद्राक माजर गवाय. The cat to act as a surety to the rat. Such sureties cannot be depended upon, as sooner or later they are sure to take advantage of it. "Summon not your enemy to befriend you." Cf. कांसवाक कोंबो जमान. हुंद्राच्या न्यायाक माजराची गवाय. उंदरास मांजर साक्ष.

552. हुंद्राक माल्ल्यार गणेसाक लागता. The God Ganesh gets annoyed if his riding animal—the mouse—is beaten. In fact if those in association with big people are troubled, those big people take it, as a personal affront. Cf. Prov. No. 49.

553. हुंद्राक लोखणाचो वात्र किल्याक ? Why should the rat go on nibbling iron ? Do not undertake jobs beyond your own capacity.

554. हुंद्राच्या वागान घराक उजो लायता. The foolish man sets his house on fire, to destroy the rats that infest his house.

555. हुंदीर मलाकाक गेलो. The rat has gone to Malacca Islands and returned in no way wiser. This is in reference to insignificant persons who brag about their wisdom, simply because they have visited foreign parts.

556. हुंदीर हागता किर्ते आनी शेणी थापता किर्ते ? The cowdung is dried and made into cakes for lighting fires. A man wanted to collect the dung of rats and use it in the same way. This shows crass stupidity. When the income is little, one cannot have any savings.

557. होंकल मरूं, नाजाल्यार न्हवरो मरूं; होवळ्यो रडात वर्णाक. Let the bride or bridegroom go to hell; female guests are very anxious to get their dainties. नवरा मरो कीं नवरी मरो, उपाध्याला दक्षिणेशीं कारण.

कन्या वरयते रूपं, माता वित्तम्, पिता श्रुतम् ।

बान्धवाः कुलमिच्छन्ति मिष्टान्नमितरे जनाः ।

558. हॉंकलेलीं चिन्नां वाळ्याच्या कैलार. You can judge of the bride from the way she wears her silver anklets at the wedding ceremony. A little blade shows how the wind blows. Cf. हॉंकलेलीं चिन्नां सव्यार कळटात. मुलाचे पाय पाळण्यांत दिसतात. शितावरून भाताची परीक्षा.

559. हॉंकलेलीं चिन्नां सव्यार कळटात. The bride's culture can be judged by her conduct at the marriage ceremony.